THE PATH

USING THE RELIGIONS OF THE WORLD AS A GUIDE TO PERSONAL AND SPIRITUAL DEVELOPMENT

JASON E. MARSHALL

The Path:
Using the Religions of the World as a Guide to Personal and Spiritual Development

Published By:

Stone Guild Publishing
P.O. Box 860475
Plano, TX 75086-0475
http://www.stoneguildpublishing.com/

First Paperback Edition Published 2013

ISBN-13 978-1-60532-070-0
ISBN- 1-60532-070-6

10 9 8 7 6 5 4 3 2 1

DEDICATION

This book is dedicated to my amazing wife Jessica, and my wonderful children. You all have been so patient and thoughtful during the writing process of this book, as well as loving and supportive during my numerous years as a spiritual vagabond. You have taught me the true meaning of love, and I am forever grateful.

I also dedicate this book to the brethren of Veritas Lodge No. 556 in Norman, Oklahoma. You each have played an instrumental role in adding Light to my spiritual path, and for that and so much more I am grateful.

I would also be remiss if I didn't specifically thank the following individuals who have played such an instrumental role in the writing of this book by either acting as an editor, a sounding board, or a spiritual mentor.

Matthew D. Anthony (a special thanks for the cover design)
Daniel P. Brown
Robert G. Davis
Daniel D. Hanttula
Kevin K. Main (a special thanks for editing the book)
Rustin W. Sparks
T. Brian Westmoreland

CHAPTER INDEX

THE BEGINNING

PREFACE

Since the beginning of time people have asked five fundamental questions regarding the meaning of life: "Who am I?", "What is my purpose?", "How can I find true peace and happiness?", "Is there a God, or a higher power?", and "If there is a God or higher power, how can I connect with God?". In response to these fundamental questions, great systems of thought and insight have been developed, which have become the religions of the world. While the religions of the world provide unique insights into these questions, it is still up to you to seek out the answers for yourself. These questions cannot be answered for you, because they can only be discovered by undertaking a path of personal and spiritual development that will strip away the various layers that conceal your true-self, as well as prevent you from living a happy and fulfilled life, and ultimately understanding and having a relationship with the mystery that many people simply call "God".

My search for the answers to the fundamental questions of life began in my teenage years. The religion I grew up with had its own answers to these fundamental questions, but when those answers didn't necessarily agree with my perceptions of the world, I was simply told to not question my faith, which led me to become a blind faith fundamentalist. During my undergraduate studies I took a particularly in depth course on comparative religion. This course studied many of the religions that eventually became the basis for this book, but at the time I only saw the course as another class to endure. Oh how wrong I was. Coming from a blind fundamentalist background, I had never really been exposed to any religion outside of my own faith, so for the entirety of the course I was fixated on proving to myself, and anyone that was willing to listen, how these "other religions" were wrong, and how "my religion" was the only true and correct faith. At the end of this class we were required to write a paper comparing and contrasting our personal religious philosophy with that of the world religions that we had studied. For weeks I worked on this paper that I had intended to be a *pièce de résistance* showing once and for all the superiority of my religion. However, there was a problem; I could barely get through the introductory paragraphs of the paper. No matter how many drafts I wrote, I could never get to the portions denouncing the other religions. This problem became worrisome as the deadline for the completion of the paper grew near, because I knew that the course professor, Dr. Gregory M. Scott, would not tolerate a late paper.

The night before the paper was due, I ended up having to call in sick for work so that I could focus on trying to at least turn "something" in, so that I could at least get a grade for the course. Around 3:00 am, I finally realized that I was not going to be able to finish the paper as intended. I can vividly remember that I was panic stricken at this realization, because my one goal since middle school had been to get into law school; therefore, every class, grade, and reference could be the deciding factor for whether or not I would complete my goal. In the midst of sheer panic I thought to myself, "why can't I finish this paper?", and I cried out to God for help. Then in one of the watershed moments of my life, I came to the realization that I could not finish the paper because I was being ignorant and unreasonable in my approach to the world religions. I was in effect being blinded by my own ignorance and shortsightedness. With a flood of emotion I came to the realization that every religion is trying to accomplish the same goal, just in its own unique way; therefore, there is no reason for animosity. I also realized that I had no right to denounce any religion, especially if I had not taken the time and effort to truly study what a particular religion taught with an open mind, and an open heart. After finishing the paper and the course, for which I thankfully received an A, I was determined to set out on my own journey of personal and spiritual development. I was also determined to seek out and discover Divine Truth so that I could answer the fundamental questions of life for myself, and I was willing to do whatever was necessary.

I began writing this book in 2004, after my pursuits led me to search outside of the religion that I grew up with. It is not that the religion I grew up with is bad, or somehow incomplete, but I intuitively knew that in order to find the answers I was looking for, I would have to broaden my search for Truth. During the 8 years it took to write this book, I studied the various religions of the world, and in the process I deepened my initial understanding that every religion is after the same goal. During this journey I have also been able to develop a profound sense of inner peace and happiness, as well as a real connection with God.

During my journey I have used the world religions as a kind of divine roadmap to personal and spiritual development, and I firmly believe that they can be used by anyone in their own journey. The world religions can act as a universal roadmap to divine truth because the goal of every religion is to aid the individual in understanding their true-self, and ultimately how to interact and connect with God. Every religion also teaches the importance of developing a sense of loving compassion to all of creation, even those individuals or groups that we may dislike. Putting these foundational teachings into practice cannot only help you to live a happier and more fulfilled life, but they can also better the lives of everyone by bringing about true peace and harmony. If society as a whole would only heed these simple teachings that all religions share, the wars, conflicts, and the various forms of suffering in the world would cease.

I wrote this book in the hopes that it will inspire others to explore the world religions, as well as undertake their own journey of personal and spiritual development so that they may discover their own answers to the foundational questions of life. I also hope that those who read this book will find the common thread that unites the religions of the world, as well as humanity. Therefore, I pray that you will read this book with an open mind and an open heart. I wish you well on your journey.

INTRODUCTION

We are all born, mature and develop, and eventually die. These stages of life are a few of the mile markers on the path of life that we are all continuously traveling upon. The precious gift of life that we are each experiencing can be bitter, sweet, or a combination of both, depending on our frame of mind and actions. Those who focus on cultivating a strong sense of their true nature (their true-self), and practice compassion, love, and charity will lead happy and fulfilled lives. Those who live in a state of confusion in regards to their true nature, and only strive to benefit themselves, will lead lives full of fear, anxiety, and depression, which clinical studies have shown are rampant in modern society.

The reason that most people live in a state of confusion is because most people are more concerned with the newest fashion trend, electronic gadget, celebrity faux pa, or work debacle than their own personal well being and spiritual development. All of these materialistic pre-occupations only serve to distract people from their true-self, which has no need for these things. Also these materialistic pre-occupations only bring temporary happiness and fulfillment; therefore those people caught up in this cycle are driven to accumulate more and more, in order to have the newest and the greatest, yet they never find true happiness. This is why experts have dubbed modern society a "consumer culture" rather than a "spiritual culture". In reality, the most important thing that you should focus on during your relatively brief walk down the path of life is your own personal and spiritual development. The religions of the world hold a key to this development, but you must choose to use these keys to open these doors of wisdom, which will lead to true happiness in this life, as well as in "that undiscovered country from whose bourn no traveler returns". [1]

Spiritual development involves gaining an understanding of your true-self, the world around you; and most importantly, developing a personal and meaningful relationship with the mystery that many people simply call God. Personal development involves inculcating the wisdom that you obtain into your everyday actions, so that your external actions reflect your internal refinement. The path of development is a life long journey, and it's a journey that humans have made since time immemorial. Our ancient forefathers have left a rich legacy of spiritual wisdom (divine truth) in the form of the world religions. By studying the world religions and choosing to follow the path towards personal and spiritual development, you will be following in the footsteps of the greatest teachers, sages, saints, and philosophers throughout human history. Following the path towards development can only lead to positive changes, because as a dear

---

[1] "Hamlet" – William Shakespeare

friend once told me, "There are only two mistakes that you can make on the path towards personal and spiritual development: First, never starting; and Second, not going far enough".[2]

Before you can begin your path, you must be able to distinguish truth from fact. This might seem trivial, but distinguishing between truth and fact is vitally important. Fact is something that can be proven. It is quantifiable. For example, someone can tell you that the temperature outside is 98 degrees Fahrenheit, and you could go outside with a thermometer and prove that it is indeed 98 degrees Fahrenheit outside, so therefore it would be a fact. Truth on the other hand, is something that cannot be proven. Truth is something deeply personal, and therefore, cannot be measured. For example, we know the truth that there are differences between good and evil, because we can feel the difference; however, there is no machine that can measure the difference between good and evil. The most important truth, love, also cannot be measured. Everyone loves someone else, whether it is your parents, spouse, children, co-workers, friends etc.; however, there is no way to quantifiably measure the amount of love that you have, and thereby prove that you love someone. We just know love because we feel it; we experience it on a deeply personal level. In the same way, God's Divine Truth cannot be measured or quantified; it must be felt and experienced on a deeply personal level. The world religions provide the keys to Divine Truth which will unlock true happiness, as well as allow you to directly commune with God;

---

[2] Rustin Sparks

however, you must be able to determine what is divine truth, and what is merely man-made dogma.

The various religions of the world attempt to facilitate divine communion with God; however, unfortunately, religious dogma can interfere with Divine Truth. Blind adherence to religious dogma can cause our focus to be taken off of true communion with God, and instead direct our focus towards the ego and self-gratifying practices. Dogma is the physical manifestation of faith, such as doctrine, the styles and practices of worship, etc., so it is man-made. It is not Divine Truth. Too often, people get so caught up in the dogmatic practices of their faith that they lose sight of what is most important, and that is their personal relationship with God, which can cause them to never fully experience God's love in a personal and meaningful way.

Blind adherence to religious dogma has also led many people into the false belief that they are in possession of the only "true religion", and that somehow they are the only people who have the keys to the gates of heaven. This of course cannot be true if you believe that God has created everything in the universe, including every living being. If God created every living being, then every living being is a child of God, and God would not condemn or abandon one of his children in favor of another, especially over something as trivial as what name you call God by, or your particular style of worship, which are matters that most "religious people" quibble over.

Unfortunately, at any time you only have to turn on the television to see news coverage of how followers of one religion or religious sect are engaged in a conflict with members of a different religion or sect. It is a travesty that millions of people have been slaughtered in the name of religion. The slaughtering and persecution of our fellow man goes directly against the message of Divine Truth that God has provided for us via the various world religions. The Crusades, the Inquisitions, and modern Islamic terrorists, are just a few examples of how religion has been used as a tool of oppression and conquest. The Christian Crusades through the "Holy Land" brought death and destruction in the name of God and Jesus Christ, which is ironic because the bloodshed of the Crusades went directly against the message of peace and love that Jesus Christ taught. The Inquisitions were fueled by religious zealotry and a thirst for power and control, which again went against the teachings of love and tolerance that Jesus taught. The modern Islamic terrorists have been indoctrinated into a false view of Islam by leaders who wish to gain media attention in order to realize their political goals, which have nothing to do with the teachings of Muhammad, yet blood is continuing to be spilt in the name of the religion that he founded. There are less obvious conflicts that are caused by religion every day which include harassment, mistrust, and discrimination towards people who do not share a particular individual's or group's religious views.

Religion itself is not bad, because spiritual practices are an essential way to realize a connection with God in this physical realm and beyond; however, religion should always be used as a tool for spiritual growth, and never as a weapon. The ill deeds and bad acts done in the name of religion are generally caused by people who highjack a religion for personal motives, or by ignorant followers who do not know the true message and nature of their own religion. The hijacking of religion is often done by people who want to use religion as a platform to further their own personal motives. They just clothe their motives in religious attire, and these people tend to be the religious radicals. Religious hijackers are successful because people tend to blindly follow the charismatic leaders who preach doomsday scenarios, or profess that they are God's sole mouthpiece with the only keys to the gates of heaven. After all, not many people want to argue with someone who claims to be God's sole mouthpiece, and everyone wants to be on a winning "team". These religious hijackers cause problems because not only do people blindly follow their orders, edicts, rulings, etc., but they indoctrinate followers and future leaders who will continue to spread their false brand of religion far into the future. Ignorant religious followers are those who have been indoctrinated into a false view of their religion by a religious hijacker, or those who have simply not taken the steps to truly study and learn about the true nature of their religion. These ignorant religious followers do not have a true "base" or understanding regarding their religion. These ignorant religious people cause problems, because when they feel a threat to their myopic religious viewpoints, they tend to become defensive and make rash decisions which can have far reaching consequences.

During your journey towards personal and spiritual development you will discover that God's true nature is pure love, pure light, pure joy, and that his loving energy permeates all of creation. You will also discover that you are a unique creation of God, yet on an ultimate level you are interrelated with all of God's creations. You are interrelated with all of God's creations because every living being has been given a "divine spark" by God, which is the energy that animates every living being. This divine spark, or true-self, goes by various names depending on tradition: atman, soul, subtle mind, etc., and will be used interchangeably in this book. What name you call this divine spark is unimportant because each name is referring to the same thing, which is the purest form of "you", that also connects "you" to God. This divine spark is a precious gift because it allows you to directly commune with God, and it is also the only thing that will survive the inevitable death of your physical body. Therefore, you must make the conscious choice to discover and cultivate your true-self, which will allow you to connect with God in this life, as well as in whatever awaits each of us after death.

The overall premise of this book is to discuss the Divine Truth that lies at the heart of the various religions of the world, and show how their teachings can be applied to one's personal path of development. This means going past the dogmatic teachings that have been built up around religion over the millenniums, which so often lead to strife, and focusing solely on Divine Truth, which is a message of peace and love meant to unite humanity, not divide us. Divine Truth is the golden thread that unites all of the world religions into a beautiful tapestry, that when taken as a whole, can begin to show the face of God.

God has sent humanity the various world religions, in order to light our way on the path towards spiritual development. By studying the teachings of the world religions with an open mind and heart you will begin to gain a clearer picture of not only yourself and the world around you, but you will also gain a clearer picture of God. This book will discuss Christianity, Judaism, Islam, Hinduism, Buddhism, Taoism, and Confucianism. However, these are only a small glimpse at the beautiful tapestry of religions that mankind has woven in its pursuit of God.

A few housekeeping matters for this book are worth noting. First, for brevity and to avoid redundancy, instead of stating "the path of/towards personal and spiritual development", simply "The Path" will generally be used. Second, every religion has its own name for God, but for the sake of clarity, this book will primarily use the name "God", in order to prevent confusion. Third, God is both masculine and feminine in nature, but again, for uniformity and simplicity the pronoun "he", will be used. Fourth, the "A.D." dating system that is generally used in the west is based off of Christianity, where A.D. (*Anno Domini*) stands for, "in the year of our Lord", and B.C. stands for, "Before Christ"; therefore, out of universal respect for all religions, and because it is generally used in academic settings, B.C.E., "Before the Common Era", will be used. Finally, the goal of this book is not to make you an expert on these religions, but to give you a synopsis of the teachings of the major world religions and show how they can be used to answer the fundamental questions of life, enhance your personal path, and ultimately develop a real connection with the mystery of God.

REFLECTION

Is there a God?

Before beginning The Path you must first understand and accept that there is a spiritual realm, as well as some sort of higher power in the universe. After all, it doesn't make much sense to be actively seeking The Path if you don't believe that there is some sort of higher power or a spiritual realm. It should be noted that it doesn't matter what "model" or "form" of God you believe in, nor is it important what name you call "God" by. In order to undertake The Path, it is only important that you believe in some form of a higher power. What God is, or isn't, will be revealed to you in a personal way as you undertake your path.

Many people who lack faith in God say that God has never spoken to them; or that he hasn't bailed them out of their problems, even self-inflicted problems like drug abuse, bad relationships, and poor lifestyle choices. The response to that is "have you been listening?" Not only does God exist, but he communicates with each of us through the soul, which acts as a direct line of communication with God. The soul is God's greatest gift to humanity, because it not only allows us to experience God, but it also allows us to actually have a direct relationship with God. Everyone knows the feeling in the pit of your stomach, or the "little voice in your head", before you do something good or bad, or when you are about to make a major decision; that feeling is your soul telling your "active self" what you should do. Now then, whether or not you listen to your soul and follow God's plan is entirely up to you; however, if you do not listen to your soul, then you cannot say that God didn't try, or even worse that God has somehow abandoned you, anymore than you can blame a TV for not working when you have refused to turn it on.

God also reveals himself in the form of miracles that constantly surround us, many of which easily go unnoticed. For example, earth and its numerous "systems" that help support the huge diversity of life are miracles (made up of a combination of countless miracles) that can easily go unnoticed. The intricacy of these systems, and how one system builds upon another in just the right way, at the very least, proves the existence of a divine force. To illustrate, our planet is the perfect distance from the sun to provide just the right amount of heat to support the huge diversity of life on earth. If earth were closer to the sun it would be too hot to have the large amount of liquid water necessary to support a wide variety life. If earth were further away from the sun, the temperature would be too cold, and water would simply remain frozen, and unable to support a wide variety of life. Our planet is also just the right size to hold together our delicate atmosphere, which contains the perfect amount of life supporting gases, including the ozone layer that protects life from the sun's harmful radiation. Our planet also revolves around the sun in an orbit which, with the aid of the 23 degree tilt in the earth's axis and various gravitational forces, provide for the daytime/nighttime, cyclical weather, and seasonal patterns. All of these life-supporting systems work together according to God's divine plan to not only support life, but help it flourish. It could be a coincidence, or chance, that a few of these life supporting factors could occur together; however, taken as a whole, the earth and its various life supporting systems are miracles that prove the existence of God.

Life itself is the most amazing miracle of all, and one that is too often taken for granted. All materials in the universe are composed of simple elements; however, what separates you from a rock is not only your composition of the simple elements, but the divine spark that gives you life. Atheists contend that life on earth sprang out of the rich "primordial soup" of our early planet which happened to contain all of the necessary elements for life. However, brilliant scientists have tried their best, yet they have never "created" life simply out of elements, even under perfect laboratory conditions. The best that science can currently do is copy and/or manipulate the genes and cells of something that has already been given the divine spark from God. Even the simplest organisms have this divine spark that gives life. Without the divine spark there is no life, only a universe of basic elements. This doesn't mean that evolution doesn't exist, nor does it mean that various other scientific theories are incorrect. The miracle of life simply shows that, at the very least, some form of God exists, and that God has given the divine spark to animate what would otherwise simply be a universe of basic elements.

The formation of a human child is also a miracle, and of course one that is especially important to anyone reading this book. The formation of a human child from conception to birth shows just how precise God is, and just how strong the divine spark is within us. Just the act of conception is a miracle in itself. In order for conception to occur the mother must release a healthy egg that she has been carrying for her entire life, and then the father's sperm must reach the egg within the narrow 24 hour period in which the egg is receptive to fertilization. Once the egg is fertilized, the separate strands of DNA from each parent must then intertwine perfectly to form the approximately 3 billion base pairs that go into the 46 chromosomes that compose human DNA. While the fetus grows and develops, organs and trillions of cells, nerve endings, blood vessels, etc. must all form correctly, and at just the right time. The formation of a child is a bit overwhelming when you take into account the trillions upon trillions of factors that go into it, and just how delicate this whole process truly is, and how much can go wrong. However, research has shown that approximately 97% of all children are properly formed and born healthy. The divine spark from God is what fuels the transformation from simple sperm and egg into a living child. The framework that God has put into place allows the various biological steps to take place in the correct order, and at the correct time.

Science has come far in explaining how life and the universe operate. These scientific discoveries have shown just how delicate and intricate life and the universe are. However, instead of disproving God, they actually show the existence of some kind of creator. The whole universe operates like an amazing clock, with each intricate solar system, planet, star, black hole, etc. acting like a small cog in the overall design. God's will to create is what created the universe, and God's will to create is what is driving the evolution of the universe, as well as life on earth. By understanding science, you can peel back the watch cover of this reality and truly begin to see the face of God. In the end, science and religion are both after the same goal, and that is to understand how the universe works, and what our role in the universe is. As Albert Einstein said, "Science without religion is lame, and religion without science is blind".

It is important to note that during your journey on The Path, the model or form of God that is revealed to you may be very different from the "traditional" model or form, or the form that is known by someone else, or even the form that you used to believe in. The differences in people's perception of God are due to each individual's unique life experiences, as well as how far along The Path they are. Also, God's true form can never be fully known, because God is so vast that the human mind cannot fully grasp the scope of God, so individual understanding and experiences will vary. However, by undertaking the path towards spiritual development, you will learn to embrace this mystery that we call God, and truly experience his love, in whatever form God reveals himself to you.

Preparing for Spiritual Development

Inscribed above the entrance to the Greek temple of Apollo at Delphi was the saying, "Man know thyself, and thou will know the universe and the gods". This ancient wisdom points to the fact that it is essential to understand your true-self, because without an accurate picture of your true-self it is impossible to gain true insight into the mysteries of God. After all, trying to comprehend the mystery that is God without a complete picture of your true-self would be like trying to view the world through a pair of dirty eye glasses. Knowing your true-self requires that you understand your psyche, which is composed of the various parts of your conscious and unconscious self. The various parts of your psyche are what drive your needs, desires, feelings, prejudices, and beliefs, as well as how you view and relate to God. Therefore, in order to truly progress on The Path you must understand, harness, and balance the often competing subparts of your psyche.

Since the 19th Century the science of psychology has made many advances that allow us to peer within the human mind in order to understand the human psyche and harness the true potential

that is contained within each of us. In many ways the concepts that
have been developed by leading psychologists mirror the concepts
and teachings within the various world religions. For example, many
of the modern psychological models recognize the existence of different levels within the human conscious and unconscious mind, and
that these levels must be explored and brought into harmony in order
to realize your full potential. These concepts are mirrored by many
of the symbols and teachings of the world religions, especially in the
Kabbalistic tree of life symbol, as well as in the Hindu concept of the
Chakras. In the context of spiritual growth, each Sephirah on the tree
of life, and each Chakra, are said to be composed of energy centers
representing a different aspect of your soul which must be properly
harnessed in order to realize your full spiritual potential.

Dr. Sigmund Freud (1856-1939) believed that the human
psyche (personality) was divided into the "Id", "Ego", and "Superego". In Dr. Freud's scheme the "Id" is the only subpart of your
psyche that is present at birth. The Id is entirely unconscious, and it
controls your basic primal thoughts and emotions. The Id seeks out
the immediate gratification of all of your desires, wants, and needs.
When your desires, wants, and needs are not immediately satisfied,
the Id induces states of anxiety, fear, stress and even anger. The Id
is an especially powerful force in children, which explains why very
young children will become upset and cry when even a basic desire
is not immediately met. The Ego is the subpart of your psyche that
deals with the every day world. The Ego functions in both the conscious and unconscious mind, and forms much of the persona that

you present to the world. The Ego acts as a filter for the Id to ensure that your needs are met, yet in a more socially acceptable and even-tempered manner. The Ego also acts as a filter for the highest part of your psyche, the Superego. The Superego is the part of your psyche that forms your morals standards, and ideals. The Superego is the part of your psyche that determines your beliefs, prejudices, ideals and goals. Dr. Freud believed that in order for a person to realize their full potential they must explore these various parts of their psyche and find a balance between the often-competing forces of the Id, Ego, and Superego. If a person is unbalanced, they may experience various psychological and social issues. For example, an unbalanced person may give into the desires of Id, which may lead to addictive behavior, or they may be inclined to give into the Superego, which may lead someone to be too unrealistic and unable to achieve goals.

Dr. Carl Jung (1875-1961) was a colleague of Dr. Freud who developed his own model of the human psyche after disagreeing with several parts of Freud's model. Dr. Jung's model is similar to Dr. Freud's model with the addition of several features, most of which are well beyond the scope of this book. In short, Dr. Jung believed that the human psyche was composed of a "Personal Unconscious Mind", a "Collective Unconscious", and "Archetypes" which are composed of "The Shadow", "Anima/Animus", and the "Self". The Personal Unconscious Mind basically composes the same subparts of the psyche as Freud's model, and is what most of us naturally think of when we think of the unconscious mind. The Collective Unconscious is a part of your unconscious that is inherited by, and is possessed by, the whole of humanity. The Collective Unconscious helps human-ity form basic ideas and symbol interpretations that are consistent throughout the various world cultures. The Archetypes are concepts or models that are hardwired into the unconscious and include The Shadow, Anima/Animus, and the Self. The Shadow is composed of the parts of your psyche such as thoughts, tendencies, and even tal-ents that you have repressed as a defense mechanism, because you view them as unacceptable. The Anima/Animus is the part of your psyche that is normally associated with the opposite gender (popular culture refers to this as our masculine/feminine sides). The Anima is the feminine archetype for men, and the Animus is the masculine ar-chetype for women. The Anima/Animus has a tremendous influence, on how you conceive your sexual role in society, as well as who you choose as a partner, because people are generally attracted to those who closely resemble their Anima/Animus. Finally, the Self is the ar-chetype that lies at the center of the conscious and unconscious self, and represents the integration point of the human psyche. The Self is what people are generally referring to when they think of "I". Jung believed that each person has an innate desire and drive to explore and balance the various parts of our psyche, which when properly performed, allow individuals to become self-realized. If a person does not become self-realized, the various parts of the psyche will compete for control, and neurotic symptoms such as depression, anxiety, pho-bias, addictive behavior, etc. can occur.

Dr. Abraham Maslow (1908-1970) believed that humans have five basic needs, which he ordered into his famous hierarchy of needs. The hierarchy of needs begins with the most primitive needs, and once those needs are met, people should naturally proceed onto the next level of needs, until finally realizing the final stage of "Self-actualization". The most primitive needs are the "Physiological Needs", which are things that the physical body requires like food, water, and sleep. Once the primitive Physiological Needs are taken care of people naturally seek out the next level, which are the "Safety Needs", which include security of the body, resources, property, and health. The next level of need is "Love and Belonging", which includes the need to feel love and a sense of belonging to groups such friends, family, society as a whole, and even sexual intimacy with our partners. The fourth level of needs deals with "Esteem", and includes selfesteem, achievement, confidence, and the need to be respected by others, as well as respect others. The final and highest need has to do with "Self-actualization", which involves morality, problem solving, and creativity. The desire to seek out God also falls under Self-actualization and seems to be a basic human need. After all, various concepts of God seem to have been around as long as man has, and these ideas have continued to evolve throughout human history as societies have changed.

In today's global society most people have their basic needs met, which should mean that more individuals are obtaining the highest levels of development, and that society as a whole is becoming more advanced and harmonious. However, as evidenced by the high rates of depression and addiction, most people are not finding balance and integration in the Freud and Jung models, and are therefore not moving into the Selfactualization stage of Maslow's model. The high rates of depression and addiction in our society are due in large part to the fact that instead of striving to find balance, and become self-realized, too many people are content with simply staying at the Love and Belonging and Esteem stages in Maslow's model. Also, many people are not finding balance, or moving towards Self-Actualization because it is much easier to simply take a pill and continue to repress memories, thoughts, beliefs, and prejudices rather than directly deal with them.

Many people are also content with feeding the lowest part of the human psyche, what is generally termed outside of psychology simply as "the ego" (not necessarily the Freud concept). The ego is the part of your psyche that leads you to be self-centered, and feel self-important. The ego segregates and suppresses your true-self from God and the world around you. In order to find your true-self you must tame your ego, and bring it into balance. This can be a difficult undertaking to accomplish, because many people build their ego up around themselves like a wall, which they use to protect them from any discomfort by telling themselves, "I am better than _____", or "I don't care what 'they' think", etc. Many people also need to "feed" their ego, just like a drug addict, shopping addict, sex addict, or any other addict needs to feed their addiction first and foremost (these addictions are caused by the ego to begin with). The stripping away of the ego in order to bring it into balance will reveal many of the pains and insecurities that have long been buried by the ego, which can be a painful process. However, this work must be done, because the ego, if left unchecked, is the antithesis of spiritual development.

Therefore, the ego must be properly channeled in order for spiritual development to occur.

A properly channeled ego is present in a spiritually developed person, because a truly spiritually developed person is not concerned with the things that the ego feeds off of such as public praise, money, material objects, and power. The reason that a spiritually developed person is not concerned with the desires of the ego is because the things that the ego feeds off of are only temporary; when you die your earthly possessions will eventually turn to dust, your legacy will most likely be forgotten by future generations, and any addictions which consumed your life will have been meaningless wastes of energy and time. A spiritually developed person is not concerned with things that only give temporary happiness; rather, by discovering their true-self, they have unlocked lasting happiness.

By exploring and finding balance between the often-competing subparts of your psyche, you will truly discover who "you" truly are. By becoming self-realized you will become comfortable in your own skin, which makes you truly powerful because you will no longer seek the praise of others in order to make yourself feel good. By becoming self-realized, you will no longer be at the mercy of what others think about you, because you will love yourself no matter what others may think. You will also be able to put your desires, worries, and thoughts into perspective. During this process you will also find that many of the activities and worries that used to consume your life have lost importance. You will find that the simple things in life such as family and friends, have much more meaning, and things like television, work, gossip, and material possessions have far less importance.

By finding balance, you will also positively affect the world around you. As you become more balanced, and more self-realized, the world around you will also become more balanced. This is because the laws of cause and effect operate in our personal and spiritual lives, so balance creates balance, and chaos creates chaos. Therefore, the inner ripples of peace that you create within yourself will manifest in the world around you, in the same way that ripples move outward on the surface of a pond after a stone is thrown in.

You can move towards self-realization by simply slowing down and practicing relatively simple daily tasks such as a short prayer of thankfulness, a moment of reflection, a quiet meditation, or simply putting the wisdom contained in the ancient scriptures into practice by performing acts of love, compassion, and kindness upon other living beings. Doing these simple acts everyday will help to change how you think about the world and your place in it. Simply slowing down to fully experience and appreciate life is reflected in one form of Buddhist meditation, where concentration is put on the simple act of breathing, which can be used to remind us that every breath that we take is a gift from God, and is something that should not be taken for granted, or wasted.

Of all his creations, God gave humans the precious gift of reason. By pursuing an active path towards personal and spiritual development you will put this gift of reason to use. In order to use the gift of reason, you must confront and examine your beliefs, life experiences, and the various parts of your psyche. This can be uncomfortable because you will have to examine tough subjects, many of which you have probably never truly examined. Also, after truly examining yourself and your beliefs, you will probably change many long held beliefs, which may mean that you no longer fit into a tidy social or religious box. However, this work is necessary because as Socrates famously said, "an unexamined life is not worth living".

DIFFERENT TAKES ON GOD

DIFFERENT "RELIGIONS" SAME GOD

Many people tend to think that their religion is somehow superior to all other religions; and therefore, that their "God" is superior to another's "God", which I call the "God Superiority Complex". This is a foolish position to take if you really believe that God created the entire universe, and therefore every person who has ever lived on this planet. Archeologists estimate that modern humans have been on earth for approximately 200,000 years. In Contrast, the oldest currently practiced religion, Hinduism, can only trace its roots back to approximately 3,500 years ago, which equates to approximately 1.75% of human history. So even if you take the oldest religion's view on God as exclusively correct (Hindus do not make this claim), that means that God left humanity in the dark for approximately 98.25% of human history. If you believe that Jesus was the one and only true incarnation and teacher of God's wisdom, that percentage jumps to 99%. Therefore to believe that any modern concept of God is totally complete, infallible, and exclusively correct is naive. To believe so would mean that "God" purposefully abandoned the vast majority of the human race for the vast majority of history, which is nonsensical.

God would not abandon any group of his children, and he has not changed the "rules" which would allow a modern religion to "now" be the only correct way.

Many people with a God Superiority Complex are reluctant to change, adapt, or expand their beliefs, because instead of truly exploring themselves, the world around them, and truly seeking out God, it is far easier to blindly cling to a religious system. Karl Marx famously stated that, "religion is the opiate of the masses". In many ways this is a true statement, because it is easy for people to simply attach themselves to a religious system where they can be spoon fed spiritual teachings at religious services, and only be required to go through the motions of devotion.

The problem with this kind of religious mentality is that it leads to a vast amount of people who are ignorant about not only their religion, but about themselves. It is alarming how many people profess to be devoted followers of a particular religious creed, yet when asked if they have read their holy books in their entirety, they cannot truthfully answer that they have. However, many of these people are more than willing to quote that which they have been told over and over again in a religious service, yet knowing nothing of its original context, or true meaning.

This type of religious ignorance is dangerous, because it breeds fundamentalism and extremism, which have been the cause of far too much strife and bloodshed. Several studies have even shown that generally the more "fundamental" a person is in regards to their re-ligion, the more ignorant they really are about their own religion, as

well as the other world religions. These religiously ignorant funda-
mentals are basically undertaking their spiritual path with a pair of
blinders on to such an extent that they have lost sight of their own
religion. Since they have also never undertaken any meaningful in-
trospection, these people do not have a clear picture of their true-self,
which is why these people tend to have high rates of depression and
anxiety. This really precludes them from living a happy and fulfilled
life or having a meaningful connection with God.

People with a God Superiority Complex also tend to wear their
religion on their sleeve, as a sort of badge of honor. They use religion to elevate themselves in society or within their religious group,
which helps to feed their egos. These people also use religion as a
way of separating themselves from other people, which develops into
an "us" versus "them" mentality when it comes to people from different groups, cultures, religions, etc. This could be a throwback to
tribal times when you justifiably needed to be suspicious of outsiders
("them"). As a result, these people naturally tend to pride themselves
on the merits of "us", while downplaying, or outright dismissing, the
merits of "them". This tribal mentality directly correlates to many
people's feelings about "other religions" and "other Gods", because
these people, either consciously or unconsciously, look at other religions as a sort of threat to their own religion, and therefore classify
other religions as wrong or somehow evil.

The God Superiority Complex directly goes against the most
basic belief that every religion holds, which is that God created everything in the universe, including every living being. If you believe

that this is true, then why is it so hard to believe that God has shown himself to every culture at different times and in different ways throughout the ages? Why is it such a hard stretch of the imagination to believe that all of the different religions throughout the world have "it" at least partly right, and can therefore impart some wisdom? God, the creator of the universe, did not create the universe in order to leave humanity in the dark for most of its existence. God created the universe and humans out of a loving desire to create. This loving desire to create is what still allows life and the universe to continue existing and expanding. God created humans to interact and connect with him, and every culture has done so in its own unique way. God doesn't take offense to the various styles of worship, because, like a parent, he instructs each of his children a little differently and in a way that they can comprehend, yet he still loves each of his children unconditionally.

The various religions throughout human history have developed because humans have sought to reconnect with God in the best way that they could understand. "Religion" is a group's view of God within their own contextual understanding of their world. For example, to the ancient cultures whose survival hinged on the various seasons, the success of the harvest, the fertility of their people, etc., it was natural to assign certain entities or Gods to these important issues. Their view of God would make sense to a group of people who lived in such close harmony with nature that their survival literally depended on nature's bounty. Another example is the ancient Jewish people who envisioned God as an entity that guided his people out of the land of Egypt, and also led them to great and often miraculous victories on the battlefield. This protective God made sense to a people who had just escaped from bondage and needed strength and courage to fight off the various people who were already living in the land they wished to make their own. To the early Christians, having a savior who would deliver them from the oppression of the Roman Empire made sense. This is not to say that these religions were wrong or somehow misled, because the people who began these religions where simply viewing God according to their understanding of the world.

As human awareness and understanding of the world has increased, religion has been forced to change and adapt, often with considerable growing pains. For example, the understanding of astronomy has changed to such an extent that the Catholic Church has been forced to rescind its view that the earth is flat and at the center of the universe. If you had espoused a belief such as that 300-400 years ago you would likely have found yourself imprisoned, like Galileo Galilei, or even killed as a heretic.

Since no religion is exclusively correct, or truly complete, no religion can have a monopoly on the soul. The soul is a unique and separate entity from religion. Religion provides a path towards knowledge and truth, yet not following a certain religious system or practice does not damn a soul to hell. By consciously or subconsciously rejecting God, who is the creator of the universe, the individual person will be damning themselves to a present existence, as well as an afterlife, of their own making. All religions agree that it is your actions here on earth that will determine your place in the after life. This is why it so important for each person to embark on a lifelong journey of personal and spiritual development. Religion provides the framework that you can use to embark on your journey, but no single religion can claim to posses the only keys to heaven. When you break down the various religions into their most foundational aspects; the fundamental teachings are all the same. The core teachings are all about love, compassion, and harmony between humanity and God. By looking at various religious teachings you can gain different perspectives and insight into God.

The differences between the world religions should not be cause for strife. Religion should be a tool for clarification and spiritual development, because it enables us to gain different insights into Divine Truth, which allow us to develop a clearer picture of our true-self and God. For example, if you show your hand to someone standing in front of you (palm side facing them) and ask them to describe your hand, you will probably get an answer dealing with the color, the fact that there are lines, a band of precious metal might be visible, etc. Now then, if someone is standing behind you, and you ask them to describe your hand they would describe fingernails, knuckles, perhaps precious stones adorning your rings (the individual to your front could only see the band portion), etc. Now then, who is correct? Is the visualization of the person in front of you wrong? Is the person behind you wrong? Of course not. Both people are correct; however, their descriptions are incomplete. Since each person could only view your hand from their present position, they could only describe it in a way that conformed to their viewpoint. If both people worked together and compared their unique view of your hand, they would get a much clearer picture of your hand that would be much closer to the true likeness of your hand. In the same way, we should work together and not be afraid to look at other religions in order to gain a more complete picture of God.

The following chapters will explore the religions that approximately 90% of "religious people" in the world follow. These religions are full of Divine Truth, which will aide any spiritual seeker in their journey along The Path. Please read the following chapters with an open mind and an open heart. These chapters will discuss the basic beliefs of each major religion that has been selected, and will discuss how to practically apply the various teachings to your personal path.

JUDAISM

Judaism is often credited as being the first monotheistic religion. Monotheism is the view of only a single God and represents a major shift in the perception of God when compared to the pagan and polytheistic beliefs that predate monotheism by tens of thousands of years. In polytheistic religions, there are numerous gods that all interact with one another in order to explain the supernatural and natural forces of the world. In these polytheistic religions, there are numerous separate gods that control death, disease, destruction, fertility, prosperity, the weather, etc. Each of these individual gods can be worshiped by themselves, or as a whole, in order to gain their favor in a particular undertaking. Before monotheism, most polytheists also believed that their gods only had local power, and had little or no power outside of their home region. Therefore, in the ancient world when a group of people moved to a new area, or were conquered by another culture, they would simply adopt the new local gods as their own. In contrast, Monotheism believes in a single all-powerful god that created the universe and keeps the universe in balance. Monotheists don't believe that their God is limited to a particular region, because he is all-powerful and omnipresent.

According to Judaism, the ancient figure Abraham is the first person in history to actually adopt a singular God as all-powerful, which would make him the first monotheist. Abraham is considered to be the founder of the "Abrahamic" religions which are Judaism, Christianity, and Islam. The Abrahamic religions are so named because they all attempt to tie their religious roots back to Abraham. The Abrahamic religions, as you will see, place a high importance on developing a close personal relationship with God, because Abraham himself had a very personal relationship with God. Abraham is said to have even been able to speak directly to, and hear directly from, God. Abraham loved and trusted God so much that in the famous story of Abraham and Isaac, when God came to Abraham and demanded that he sacrifice his son Isaac, he actually began to comply until an angel of God stopped him at the last moment. Most biblical scholars agree that God really did not want Abraham to sacrifice Isaac; it was merely a test. The *Tanakh* is full of stories such as these, where people interacted directly with God, and God often tested their faith. Those whom God chose to test were either rewarded or punished according to their faithfulness.

The Jewish holy book, the *Tanakh* is traditionally subdivided into three separate parts containing several books. The three principle parts are: the *Torah* – "Teachings", *Nevi'im* – "Prophets", and *Ketuvim* – "Writings". These books were eventually included in the Christian *Bible* as the "Old Testament". The *Tanakh* gives a narrative history of the Jewish people and their laws and customs from their creation story to approximately 425 B.C. Overall, the *Tanakh* gives a detailed narrative about the Jewish people's close and intimate relationship with God, as well as the inherent struggles and pitfalls associated with such a close relationship. For example, the *Tanakh* outlines that the Jewish people often struggled to live up to the covenants that they made with God, and God punished these breaches with varying degrees of severity. This highlights the fact that as you gain greater knowledge of your true-self and God, you will take on greater responsibilities, and you will suffer if you fail in those responsibilities.

Some of the covenants that the Jewish people made with God required them to make various ritual sacrifices to God. These sacrifices had to be the best of whatever was being sacrificed, be it animal or some sort of crop. This signified the person's devotion to God, because they were willing to give up the very best of what they had. While most modern people might look at this practice as strange, wasteful, or even foolish, it is not so strange when you think about the fact that everything we have, in fact everything in the universe, is a gift from God. Therefore, making a sacrifice to God was simply a way of thanking God for his many gifts and blessings. While some of the ancient people believed that God somehow "consumed" (ate or drank) the sacrifices, what was more important was the action of giving thanks to God by permanently giving up something important to you. Today we can thank God for his many gifts and blessings by practicing charity. By practicing charity we are giving up something that we could easily keep and use for our pleasure; however, by practicing the act of charity, we are thanking God for his many blessings, and the charitable gift is being used to better someone else's life. Today, Jews no longer make ritual sacrifices, because Jewish law mandates that all sacrifices be made at the Jewish Temple in Jerusalem, the last version of which was destroyed by the Romans in 70 A.D.

Modern Judaism has several different sects ranging from Hasidic, Orthodox, Reformed, to Kabbalistic; therefore, constructing a clear and concise view of Jewish beliefs and practices can be difficult. Also, as a whole, Judaism is much more concerned with actions, rather than beliefs. However, according to the medieval Jewish philosopher Moses Maimonides, there are thirteen principles of the Jewish faith. Like the Nicene Creed for Christians, not all Jews believe in or follow all of Maimonides thirteen principles; however, these thirteen principles are fairly universal, and have generally been identified as foundational requirements for the Jewish faith. Therefore, for the purposes of this book, exploring the thirteen principles of faith as laid down by Maimonides, and applying them to The Path will work well. According to Maimonides, the thirteen principles of Jewish faith are as follows:

1. To know the existence of God
2. God's unity
3. God's spirituality and nonphysicality
4. God's eternity
5. God alone should be the object of worship
6. Revelation through God's prophets
7. The preeminence of Moses among the prophets
8. God's law was given on Mount Sinai

9. The immutability of the Torah as God's Law
10. God's foreknowledge of human actions
11. Reward of good and retribution of evil
12. The coming of the Jewish Messiah
13. The resurrection of the dead.

The first principle, to know the existence of God, is an absolute necessity for someone embarking on The Path. It is important to realize and appreciate that God, in whatever form, is the only reason that this universe and all of its mysteries exist. He created everything in this universe, and he is the balancing force that keeps everything in order. In the modern world it is often too easy to become detached from our surroundings and God, because we are constantly bombarded with technological and social distractions. These distractions in our lives build an artificial wall that separates us from God and also desensitizes us. If we would just take a few moments each day to just relax, clear our minds, and reflect (meditate) on the many blessings of God, the artificial wall that we have created between God and ourselves will dissolve away. Once the artificial wall between ourselves and God is removed we can then commune with God as he has intended.

> *"And you will love the Lord your God with all your heart and with all your soul and with all your strength"* [1]

The second principle, God's unity, goes hand-in-hand with the first principle, because once you realize that there is a God who has

---

[1] Deuteronomy, 6:5

created the universe, and everything in it, then it is inevitable to come to the conclusion that God must be connected to everything, be it a plant, an animal, or any substance in the universe. There is literally nothing in this universe that can be separate from God, because God created everything to begin with. This does not mean that everything "is" God, but God is connected to all of his creations, just as a parent is connected to their children. Even God's non-living creations are still formed from the substances that God has created and are governed by the physical laws that he put into place. God has provided all living things with the divine spark, which gives it what we know as "life". The child which grows in the mothers womb has it, the tree outside your window has it, even the most vile person you can think of has it. They have simply chosen to not realize this fact and embrace the gift that God has given them. The key is to seek out God and truly feel his love and energy in every moment of your life.

> *"Then you will begin to seek God your Lord, and if you pursue Him with all your heart and soul, you will eventually find Him."* [2]

The third principle, God's spirituality and nonphysicality, basically means that God is purely a spiritual force, he is the essence of creation. Most Westerners picture God as some sort of older Santa Clause like figure riding on a cloud, with a "naughty and nice list". The modern depictions of God in the western world are basically taken from the ancient Greek depictions of Zeus, and are unrealistic.

---

[2] Deuteronomy, 4:29

Basically, when we picture God in this way we are applying human attributes to him, which is always false because God is beyond human form. When we begin to picture God as some sort of superhuman, then it is natural to apply our human emotions to him. This is why most people believe that we can somehow anger God, or make God vengeful. The truth is that you cannot anger God, because God's ultimate form is pure love, pure energy. If you choose to go against and reject God's universal love, negative things may happen to you, but not because God is angry with you. You may suffer because once you choose to reject God's love, you inevitably align yourself with negative influences that often lead to some sort of destructive behavior, the painful consequences of which will eventually have to be dealt with. This simple law of cause and effect is linked to the Hindu and Buddhist concept of *Karma*, which will be discussed later. To truly experience God's divine love, you must make the conscious decision to tap into his love and energy that constantly surrounds you.

> *"When I remember You on my bed, I meditate on You in the night watches, For You have been my help, And in the shadow of Your wings I sing for joy. My soul clings to You; Your right hand upholds me."* [3]

The fourth principle, God's eternity, basically means that God has always existed, and will always continue to exist. According to the Book of Genesis, God literally willed what we know as the universe and it's many levels into existence. This principle is interconnected

---

[3] Psalm 63:6-8

with the previous principles, and is a natural evolution of thought and understanding as you begin to realize the universality of God, and that his love and energy constantly surrounds each of us. God existed when our planet was nothing more than a collection of hot rock and gases orbiting a new star, and God will continue to exist once our dying sun consumes the earth at the end of its life cycle. God's love is universal and will continue to exist forever.

> *"Lord, you have been our dwelling place throughout all generations. Before the mountains were born or you brought forth the earth and the world, from everlasting to everlasting you are God. You turn men back to dust, saying, 'Return to dust, O sons of men.' For a thousand years in your sight are like a day that has just gone by, or like a watch in the night."* [4]

The fifth principle, that God alone should be the object of worship, is the belief that God is the only entity in the universe that should be worshiped. Throughout the narrative history of the Jewish people, we are told that the Jews had tendencies to revert back to pagan practices such as idol worshiping. These acts are said to have been severely punished by God because they broke the covenants that the Jews had made with God, and because these practices were taking the focus of the Jewish people away from their devotions and personal relationship with God. The traditional concept of an idol is something that is made by human hands as a physical representation of God, whose true form cannot be represented by any object, because God is

---

[4] Psalm 90:1-4

formless. Furthermore, while an idol can be burned to ash or melted down, God is eternal. In today's society many of us have replaced the physical idols of antiquity with idols such as our jobs, money, material objects, celebrities, etc. These things are unimportant because they are only temporary and transient in nature. Our jobs will be done by someone else after we retired. Money is now nothing more than a numerical value in our bank accounts that only exists in the ether of cyber space. Our material objects will all eventually fade to dust, and celebrities will age and fall out of favor, but our souls and God are eternal. Therefore, we should all strive to not allow any of these petty preoccupations keep us from focusing on our spiritual development, and ultimately on our relationship with God.

> *"...Where are their gods, the rock in which they sought refuge? Who ate the fat of their sacrifices, and drank the wine of their drink offering? Let them rise up and help you, Let them be your hiding place! See now that I, I am He, and there is no god besides Me; It is I who puts to death and gives life..."* [5]

For the purposes of this book, the sixth (Revelation through God's prophets), seventh (The preeminence of Moses among the prophets), eighth (God's law was given on Mount Sinai), and ninth (The immutability of the Torah as God's Law) principles can be discussed together. Since the Jewish faith represented a radical departure from the religions that had preceded it, these principles reflect

---

[5] Deuteronomy 32:39

the Jewish desire to protect their unique teachings and doctrines, which have been handed down through thousands of years. Like all faiths, the Jewish faith attempts to provide a roadmap to personal and spiritual development, and in order for someone to follow the Jewish faith, they must follow these foundational principles of the Jewish faith, which lay out the laws and spiritual authority of the faith. However, this does not mean that non-Jews cannot study the Jewish faith and learn from the Divine Truth contained in Judaism.

> *"You have made known to me the path of life; you will fill me with joy in your presence, with eternal pleasures at your right hand."* [6]

The tenth principle, God's foreknowledge of human actions, has often been a troublesome fact for most people to grasp. Some people have used the fact that God knows what we are going to do as an excuse to continue on with their current life path, because it must be "what God wants", or to even justify their bad actions because God would have stopped them if their actions were incorrect. The truth is that God wants us to be happy, but we still need to be proactive. Just because God may know what we are going to do does not mean that we still do not have freewill. You have the choice right now to stand on your head if you so choose. God may know that you will or will not follow through, but you still have the ability to make a choice. The fact is that God has a particular life path for you, and that is to be truly happy by communing and living in peace with not

---

[6] Psalm 16:11

only God but with the entirety of his creation. You can either choose to embrace God's love and do what God wants you to do, or you can choose to reject God's love and suffer the consequences of your own actions. Choose wisely.

The eleventh principle, Reward of good and retribution of evil, is the concept that we are awarded for our good actions, and punished for our negative actions. This concept is understood by many people in the Western world to be a sort cosmic reward and retribution system with the aforementioned Santa Clause figure sitting as judge and jury. The fact is that the most powerful force in the universe is God's love for us. As mentioned before, we can choose to accept it and embrace it, or we can choose to reject it. If we choose to follow our carnal desires, we will suffer the consequences that naturally flow from the outcomes that we have created. The world and our lives are what we make of them. We can either become tuned into God's love and affect the world in a positive way, or we can reject God's love and reap the consequences of our actions.

> *"Know therefore that the LORD your God is God; he is the faithful God, keeping his covenant of love to a thousand generations of those who love him and keep his commands."*[7]

The twelfth principle, the coming of the Jewish Messiah, is the belief that a Jewish messiah will come to deliver the Jewish people from bondage (foreign lands today), rebuild the Jewish Temple, and usher in a Messianic age. During the Messianic Age, there will be

---

[7] Deuteronomy 7:9

no crime, no war, no poverty, and the world will live in peace and harmony. The Christians believe that Jesus Christ was the Messiah, while Jews believe that he wasn't. While not discounting this belief, we each have the ability to usher in the Messianic Age. If we would all simply realize that we are all created by God and are therefore all brothers and sisters who each share the journey and mystery of life, the senseless violence, greed, and corruption in our world would cease. Since every human being carries with them the divine spark of life, the most vile deed that a person can commit is to harm another human being. The best thing that a person can do is help another human being, which is why the concept of charity is so important. If enough people would simply strive to truly co-exist and live in peace, society would begin to change, and a truly peaceful Messianic age would begin.

Finally, the thirteenth principle, the resurrection of the dead, is another controversial point, which has been adopted by the other Abrahamic religions, yet has been fiercely debated. While many followers of the Abrahamic faiths believe that the actual physical body of a deceased individual will be raised from the dead at some point in the future, our bodies are not the spiritual vehicles that will survive death. Our physical bodies are merely the vessel that currently contains the divine spark of life (our soul). The divine spark is the only thing that will survive death and move onto the next level or realm of existence. In physics, the Law of Conservation of Energy states that energy can neither be created, nor destroyed. Energy can only be transformed into another state. Since the divine spark is composed of divine energy, it will follow the laws of physics and merely transform into another state after death, but will not destroyed. The concept of physical resurrection is merely man's attempt to hold onto the physical world. The book of Genesis makes it clear that our bodies will not accompany us into the next realm of existence.

> *"By the sweat of your brow you will eat your food until you return to the ground, since from it you were taken; for dust you are and to dust you will return."* [8]

The religion of Judaism is an extremely important religion, because it appears to be the first successful monotheistic religion, and it also spawned two of the largest currently practiced religions in the world, Christianity and Islam. More importantly, Judaism is full of Divine Truth, which shows us how important it is to have a close and personal relationship with God. Judaism, especially the mystical branch known as Kabbalah, also outlines a powerful spiritual path that an individual can use to enter into a higher state of understanding. Ultimately, Judaism shows us that in order to have an intimate relationship with God, you must seek out God and change your thoughts and behaviors in order to bring them more inline with God. By following these teachings while embarking down the path

---

[8] Genesis 3:19

towards spiritual development, you will gain the knowledge that you are constantly surrounded by God's love, which is known simply as "light" in many mystical/esoteric traditions.

> *"By wisdom a house is built, and through understanding it is established; through knowledge its rooms are filled with rare and beautiful treasures."* [9]

---

[9] Proverbs 24:3-4

CHRISTIANITY

The word "Christian", which is used to denote members of the Christian faith, comes from the Greek word *Christianos*, which means "little Christ" or "followers of Christ". The term was probably first used by those who persecuted the early followers of Jesus, and was later adopted by the new Christian community as a title for their burgeoning faith. Christians follow the teachings of Jesus of Nazareth, who is more commonly known as Jesus Christ. Jesus lived around the beginning of the Common Era, which is reflected by the Julian and Gregorian calendars used in the west where A.D. stands for *Anno Domini*, which is Latin for "Year of our Lord" and B.C. stands for "Before Christ". The name "Christ" comes from Greek word *Christos*, which means "the anointed one". The term *Christos* is fitting, because according to most followers of the Christian faith, Jesus Christ was the literal son of God, who was born as a kind of sacrificial lamb to atone for the sins of man. The historical Jesus lived and taught primarily in the area known as Galilee, which is now part of modern northern Israel. Jesus is said to have begun his ministry when he was around 30 years old, and continued his ministry for approximately three years, before he was executed by the Romans via crucifixion. Although the ministry of Jesus lasted for only a brief time period, his teachings spawned the largest currently practiced religion in the world. His transformational message of peace, compassion, love, and charity is something that each person should strive to emulate.

Long before the birth of Jesus, many Jewish prophets had foretold that God would send a messiah, who would be a decedent of the biblical King David. The Jews believed that this messiah would not only rescue them from foreign rule and become King of the Jews, but that he would triumphantly show the world that they were indeed the chosen people of God and usher in a Messianic Age full of peace and prosperity. During the time when the historical Jesus lived, Israel was part of the Roman Empire, which caused many Jews to anxiously await the arrival of this prophesized Jewish Messiah. Christians believe that Jesus was the prophesized messiah, while mainstream Jews believe that he wasn't, which is the main reasons why Christianity and Judaism split into distinct religions.

Little is known about Jesus' formative years, because the traditional Gospel accounts included in the mainstream Christian canon mainly focus on his ministry and are relatively silent on his childhood, other than a few sparse passages regarding his birth and a single incident as a youth in the Temple at Jerusalem. Most biblical scholars agree that Jesus does appear to have been a well-educated Jew, who had undergone some sort of rabbinical training prior to beginning his ministry. Like the Buddha who preceded him had done with Hinduism, Jesus didn't start a new religion from scratch; rather, his teachings built upon the teachings of his background faith, Judaism. Christianity was so closely connected with Judaism that as the religion of Christianity began to grow and spread after the death of Jesus, many people simply viewed it as a new sect of Judaism. In fact, many the leaders of the early Christian church believed themselves to still be followers of Judaism and fiercely debated whether or not non-Jews (Gentiles) could become Christians without first converting to Judaism. Eventually Christianity broke away from Judaism and allowed non-Jews to join the faith; however, Christianity remained closely tied to Judaism. In fact, the Christian church eventually adopted many of the books of the Jewish faith into the Christian Bible, which became known as the "Old Testament". The selected books containing the purported biographical accounts and teachings of Jesus, as well as the teachings from the early Christian leaders, became known as the "New Testament".

Studying the historical beginnings and teachings of early Christianity can be a daunting task, because in the beginning there was no single Christian "church". Instead, early Christianity was made up of numerous small groups and sects that were largely independent of one another. Some of these various groups had dramatically different viewpoints on things such as the divinity of Jesus, what the true message of Jesus was, and what it meant to be a follower or disciple of Christ. Many of these groups also actively tried to discredit and denounce the teachings of other groups. Therefore, much of what we currently know about these early groups are from their sparse writ-

ings that survive regarding their own beliefs, as well as condemna-
tions of other groups.

The Christian Gnostics are probably the best known subsect of
early Christianity, mainly because the groups that eventually became
the dominate Catholic Church wrote extensively against their beliefs,
which were very mystical and transformative in nature. According to
the Christian Gnostics, Jesus was born as a mortal and lived a mortal's life before receiving *Gnosis* (knowledge/light/enlightenment)
through study, prayer, and meditation, much like how the Buddha is
said to have reached his enlightenment. This concept should resonate
with most people on The Path, because it means that we each have
the ability to reach a state of *Gnosis* in this current state of being,
rather than hoping only to reach such a state in the afterlife.

The various disagreements among the various early Christian
sects were threatening to tear apart the burgeoning Christian faith
until the Roman Emperor Constantine I converted to Christianity
(most likely from Mithraism), and made Christianity the Roman
Empire's semi-official religion. In order to clarify the teachings of the
Christian religion, Emperor Constantine ordered all of the leaders of
the various Christian sects to meet in a single place in order to orga-
nize and clearly define what the Christian religion was. This meeting
would become known as the 1st Council of Nicaea and met in the
year 325 AD. The Council of Nicaea and several other similar meetings of church leaders would define and shape the Christian faith
that still survives today. Out of these meetings came the foundational
concepts of modern Christianity, such as which books are officially

part of the Bible, the concept that Jesus was the literal "Son of God", the concept of the Christian trinity (God in three parts), that Jesus was a sacrificial offering to cleanse the sins of humanity, and that Jesus will return to the earth in order to judge humanity and usher in a new kingdom. Many of the concepts that were developed at the councils of Nicaea were incorporated into what has become known as the Nicene Creed, the final version of which was adopted in 381 A.D. and is as follows:

We believe in one God,
the Father, the Almighty,
maker of heaven and earth,
of all that is, seen and unseen.

We believe in one Lord, Jesus Christ,
the only Son of God,
eternally begotten of the Father,
God from God, light from light,
true God from true God,
begotten, not made,
of one Being with the Father;
through him all things were made.
For us and for our salvation
he came down from heaven,
was incarnate of the Holy Spirit and the Virgin Mary
and became truly human.
For our sake he was crucified under Pontius Pilate;
he suffered death and was buried.
On the third day he rose again
in accordance with the Scriptures;
he ascended into heaven
and is seated at the right hand of the Father.

He will come again in glory to judge the living and the dead,
and his kingdom will have no end.

We believe in the Holy Spirit, the Lord, the giver of life,
who proceeds from the Father [and the Son],
who with the Father and the Son is worshiped and glorified,
who has spoken through the prophets.
We believe in one holy catholic and apostolic Church.
We acknowledge one baptism for the forgiveness of sins.
We look for the resurrection of the dead,
and the life of the world to come. Amen.

There have been numerous changes and upheavals in Christianity since the final version of the creed was drafted in 381 C.E., including the Protestant Reformation, which spawned the Protestant sect of Christianity. While Protestant Christians do not generally recite the Nicene Creed, it is still a very good synopsis of what the majority of Christians believe. Now, compare the "Nicene Creed", which was developed over three hundred years after the death of Jesus, with that of the "Lord's Prayer", said to have actually been prayed and taught by Jesus:

This, then, is how you should pray:
'Our Father in heaven,
hallowed be your name,
your kingdom come,
your will be done
on earth as it is in heaven.
Give us today our daily bread.
Forgive us our debts, as we also have forgiven our debtors.
And lead us not into temptation,
but deliver us from the evil one.'

For if you forgive men when they sin against you, your heavenly Father will also forgive you. But if you do not forgive men their sins, your Father will not forgive your sins. [1]

Notice how much dogma is present in the Nicene Creed, when compared to the beautifully simple Lord's Prayer. The Lord's Prayer teaches us how to act, while the Nicene Creed dictates what Christians should believe. The message of the Lord's Prayer teaches the Divine Truth that we should love our fellow man unconditionally, love and have faith in God, and not become attached to the material world. Since the Lord's Prayer is said to have been actually prayed and taught by Jesus, this chapter will explore the teachings of Jesus Christ, in the context of the Lord's Prayer.

To begin with, the Lord's Prayer begins with "<u>Our</u> Father in heaven", notice that it does not start with my "<u>My</u> Father in heaven". This section alludes to the fact that since God created the entire universe, God is the ultimate father of everything in the universe. This makes each human being a child of God, which on an ultimate level makes each of us brothers and sisters. Therefore, we each must show respect to one another, and take care to not cause strife and turmoil. According to the book of Matthew, during his famous Sermon on the Mount, Jesus taught, *"You have heard that it was said to the people long ago, 'You shall not murder, and anyone who murders will be subject to judgment.' But I tell you that anyone who is angry with a brother or sister will be subject to judgment. Again, anyone who says to a brother or*

---

[1] Matthew 6:9-15

sister, 'Raca' (an Arabic term of contempt), is answerable to the court. And anyone who says, 'You fool!' will be in danger of the fire of hell." [2] If humanity as a whole would adopt the mindset that we are basically one large extended family, then the wars, conflicts, and exploitation that are rampant in our world would cease. In order to obtain and cultivate this mindset, you should strive to treat every person that you encounter with the same love, compassion, and kindness that you would show to a beloved family member or friend, even if they do not reciprocate.

The next portion, *"hallowed be your name"*, shows the reverence that Jesus paid to God. It is important to note here that Jesus did not include himself on the same level as God, instead he is plainly deferring respect to God. In his ministry Jesus made it very clear that in order to enter the kingdom of heaven, you must act according to the will of God. According to the book of Matthew, Jesus clearly stated, *"Not everyone who says to me, 'Lord, Lord,' will enter the kingdom of heaven, but only he who does the will of my Father who is in heaven. Many will say to me on that day, 'Lord, Lord, did we not prophesy in your name, and in your name drive out demons and perform many miracles?' then I will tell them plainly, 'I never knew you. Away from me, you evildoers!'"* [3]. In this passage, Jesus makes it very clear that simply professing a belief in a certain religious system is not going to be enough to grant you entrance into the kingdom of heaven. There-

---

[2] Matthew 5:21-22
[3] Matthew 7:21-23

fore, you must take care to follow the will of God in this life, and undertake whatever work is necessary to accomplish the will of God.

The next obvious question is this. What is the will of God that you must do in order to get into heaven? According to Jesus, the will of God is to love both God and your fellow man. In the book of Matthew, when Jesus was asked by one of the Pharisees what the most important commandment (law) was, Jesus replied, *"Love the Lord your God with all your heart and with all your soul and with all your mind. This is the first and greatest commandment. And the second is like it: 'Love your neighbor as yourself.' All the Law and the Prophets hang on these two commandments."* [4] You can clearly see from this quote just how important the concept of love is to the message of Jesus. Love is important, because God created the universe out of love, so love is the tie that unites humanity and the rest of creation with God. A cursory look through history shows that in the absence of love, man is capable of extraordinary cruelty; however, when love is present, man is capable of extraordinary acts of kindness. Therefore, it is important to treat each person with the love, compassion, and kindness that is due to a brother or sister created by God.

"Your kingdom come, your will be done, on earth as it is in heaven", alludes to the fact that since God has created both the physical and spiritual realms, his laws regarding love and compassion apply equally to both realms, which is why your actions in this realm carry

---

[4] Matthew 22:36-40

on with you to the next. God has created both realms. The Kingdom of God is everywhere, including within yourself in the form of your soul, which as previously discussed is the divine spark from God that animates you. According to the book of Luke, *"Once, on being asked by the Pharisees when the kingdom of God would come, Jesus replied, 'The coming of the kingdom of God is not something that can be observed, nor will people say, 'Here it is,' or 'There it is,' because the kingdom of God is within you."* [5] This is a powerful teaching, because Jesus is telling us that the kingdom of God is literally within each of us. The kingdom of God is within each of us in the form of the soul, which connects you to God, and the entirety of his creation. Therefore, in order to discover the kingdom of God in this life, you must earnestly seek out and cultivate this precious gift from God and avoid the vices and superfluities of life, which only serve to stunt your spiritual growth.

In the next few lines of the Lord's Prayer, Jesus prays to not become attached to the material world, *"Give us today our daily bread. Forgive us our debts, as we also have forgiven our debtors. And lead us not into temptation, but deliver us from the evil one."* Time and time again, Jesus warns his followers to seek out the spiritual, and stay away from the material aspects of the world. This is because the desires of the material world are never fulfilling, because no matter what material possessions we have, we will always want more. The reason that the material world is unsatisfying is that when you are in the grips of attachment, as soon as one desire is fulfilled, a new desire

---

[5] Luke 17:20-21

takes its place, so you can never have enough money or material objects. True happiness doesn't depend upon material wealth. Instead, it depends on personal and spiritual fulfillment, which is what The Path is all about.

Jesus also squarely addressed the issue of mixing money and faith when he is quoted as stating, *"No one can serve two masters. For you will hate one and love the other; you will be devoted to one and despise the other. You cannot serve both God and Money"*. [6] This passage is self-explanatory in that you cannot truly love and serve God if you are also concerned with material wealth. This is because when you focus on the material world and the accumulation of money or material objects, your attention is inevitably taken away from God and The Path. This is something that each of us struggles with on one level or another; however, you can control your desires by putting them into perspective. The easiest way to do this is to categorize your desires into "wants" and "needs". If the object of your desire is a "need", then pursue it with a level head and a clear mind. If the object of your desire is a "want", then be very cautions, and examine your motivations behind the "want". If your motivations for the "want" are wholesome, then pursue it, but make sure that you don't neglect your duties to your family, friends, or your path in its pursuit.

Jesus further elaborated on the need to not focus on material objects during his famous Sermon on the Mount, where he said, *"Don't store up treasures here on earth, where moths eat them and rust*

---

[6] Matthew 6:24

destroys them, and where thieves break in and steal. Store your treasures in heaven, where moths and rust cannot destroy and thieves do not break in and steal. Wherever your treasure is there the desires of your heart will also be"[7]. Here Jesus is telling us that our true treasure is in heaven or in the spiritual realm. All too often people tend to put wealthy people or celebrities on a pedestal and lust after their lifestyle, which drives people to try to emulate the affluent lifestyle that society expects us to portray. However, if all you do during your time here on earth is worry about the accumulation of wealth and strive to have more and more material possessions, your life here on earth will have been wasted, because your material possessions are useless to you after your death. Therefore, we need to make sure that we are not becoming attached to the material world to such an extent that we lose sight of the ultimate goal. Instead of attaching yourself to the material world, place your attention on the spiritual path where you will find lasting happiness that never becomes obsolete or goes out of fashion.

The final lines, *"For if you forgive men when they sin against you, your heavenly Father will also forgive you. But if you do not forgive men their sins, your Father will not forgive your sins"*, summarize Jesus' foundational message of unconditional love to humanity. We must strive to show the same love and compassion to humanity that God shows us daily. This means even showing love and compassion to those who have personally wronged you. According to the book of Matthew, Jesus stated, *"You have heard the law that says, 'Love your*

---

[7] Matthew 6:19-21

neighbor' and hate your enemy. But I say, love your enemies! Pray for those who persecute you! In that way, you will be acting as true children of your Father in heaven. For he gives his sunlight to both the evil and the good, and he sends rain on the just and the unjust alike. If you love only those who love you, what reward is there for that? Even corrupt tax collectors do that much. If you are kind only to your friends, how are you different from anyone else?" [8]

Surely if Jesus taught that you should love your enemies, even people who have wronged you, he would not have approved of anyone hating, belittling, or harming another person or group, especially a person or group who has not personally wronged you. Since God created each of us, when you hate or harm another person, you are ultimately hating the divine spark from God that resides in and animates that person. Therefore, you must strive to reflect love out into the world, in the same way that God constantly sends his loving energy into the world. If you feel ill will toward a person, try turning your negative emotions into positive emotions. If nothing else, realize that they are a human being, just like yourself, and as such, they at least deserve respect, even if they do not reciprocate.

The Lord's Prayer truly encapsulates Jesus Christ's message of unconditional love, compassion, and kindness between mankind and God. The teachings of Jesus are a roadmap that shows us how mankind should interact with one another, and with God. Take a moment each day and spend some time with God through prayer

---

[8] Matthew 5:43-47

and/or mediation. During this time of prayer, try to simply thank God for your many blessings, and tune into his love that surrounds you at all times. Prior to teaching them the Lord's Prayer, Jesus gave a wonderful lesson to his disciples:

> *"And when you pray, do not be like the hypocrites, for they love to pray standing in the synagogues and on the street corners to be seen by men. I tell you the truth, they have received their reward in full. But when you pray, go into your room, close the door and pray to your Father, who is unseen. Then your Father, who sees what is done in secret, will reward you. And when you pray, do not keep on babbling like pagans, for they think they will be heard because of their many words. Do not be like them, for your Father knows what you need before you ask him."* [9]

The purpose of admitting your faults during prayer should be to make a conscious affirmation that you will try to not commit those acts in the future. By also consciously making an effort to change your actions, you will bring them into alignment with the will of God. However, if you are only asking for forgiveness while knowing full well that you have no intention of modifying your behavior, you are wasting your time, as well as the tool of prayer that God has given you in order to commune with him.

Jesus' message shows how powerful unconditional love and material unattachment can be as a transformative practice. By constantly seeking to put this message into practice, you can discover

---

[9] Matthew 6:5-8

your true-self that automatically seeks to do the will of God. The reason that your true-self automatically seeks to do the will of God, is because it was created by God to begin with. Therefore, if you earnestly seek to transform your thoughts, actions, and attachments in order to bring them more in line with the Will of God, you will discover and reconnect with the divine love of God that permeates the entirety of his creation.

> *"So I say to you: Ask and it will be given to you; seek and you will find; knock and the door will be opened to you. For everyone who asks receives; the one who seeks finds; and to the one who knocks the door will be opened".* [10]

---

[10] Luke 11:9-10

ISLAM

There is currently a great deal of public and latent animosity towards Islam in the West. Much of the recent animosity stems from the modern terrorist activities of some Middle-Eastern "Islamic" groups. However, there appears to be a latent animosity that seems almost hereditary, probably due to the glorified stories that have been passed down about heroic European knights reclaiming the "Holy Land" from the "barbaric" Muslims during the Crusades, which have long been the fodder for books and movies. However, it must be remembered that the Crusades involved European armies invading the Arab world, which was actually much more intellectually and socially advanced than Europe during that time period. Modern terrorist groups are using terrorist activities as a way to strikeout against the West, which they view as oppressive and imperialistic, due in large part to numerous western invasions from the crusades to modern armed conflicts, as well as western governments meddling in Middle-Eastern politics.

While acts of terrorism should not be excused or marginalized, it must be understood that these terrorists are lashing out against the West because they feel hopeless and angry, and acts of terrorism give them a voice through news coverage. These Islamic radicals are simply using the religion of Islam as a cover story in order to pursue their goals and ambitions by portraying their actions as "God's Will", just as numerous other quasi-religious groups have done throughout history. These Islamic terrorist groups do not represent the whole of Islam any more than any radical religious group or cult represents their parent religion. The truth is that Islam is a very accepting religion and believes that at the very least, Muslims, Jews, and Christians will all go to heaven on the day of judgment.

> *"Those who believe (in the Qur'an), and those who follow the Jewish scriptures, and the Christians and the Sabians, - any who believe in God and the Last Day, and work righteousness, shall have their reward with their Lord; on them shall be no fear, nor shall they grieve."* [1]

There is a great deal of confusion among non-Muslims in the West regarding the role of Muhammad in Islam. Many Westerners believe that Muhammad was some sort of Islamic Christ figure; however, Muhammad directly rejected any notion that he was divine, he simply viewed himself as a former merchant and a prophet. Where most Christians believe that John the Baptist was the last prophet who prepared the way for Jesus; Muslims believe that Muhammad was the last profit who developed the religion of Islam through divine revelations that he received from God through the archangel

---

[1] Al-Baqarah 2:62

Gabriel. Muslims believe that Muhammad received his first revelation through Gabriel when he was 40 years old, and that he began his ministry three years later. Muhammad is responsible for developing the religion of Islam, which he did by synthesizing the teachings of Judaism, Christianity, and his own divine revelations, in a way that made them accessible and meaningful to an Arab audience.

Prior to Islam, most Arabs were pagans who believed in a multitude of Gods. By the end of Muhammad's life, much of the Middle-East had converted to Islam. It is a testament to the leadership of Muhammad and the religion of Islam itself that such a radical change in religious viewpoints was so quickly affected among the diverse Arab peoples. One of the reasons that Islam was so successful, and continues to be successful, is that Muhammad's message of peace, love, cooperation, and the need for a deeply personal relationship with God, resonates with people on a fundamental level. As with the other Abrahamic religions, these types of messages inspire people to think about and undertake actions to care for the well-being of others through compassion and charity. This facilitates the building of strong community bonds, which also naturally promote stability and growth in the society as well as in the religion.

Islam is the third major Abrahamic religion. In the same way that Christians believe that Christianity took up where Judaism left off, Muslims believe that Islam took up where Christianity left off. Islam considers itself to be a natural progression of religion that flowed from the teachings of Judaism and Christianity, which is why in the Qur'an, Muhammad calls Jews and Christians, "The People of The

Book". Muslims believe that Muhammad restored the message of God (Allah) to its true form as it had been revealed to Adam, Abraham, Moses, Jesus, and numerous other prophets and patriarchs. It is interesting to note that from a historical perspective, Judaism and Christianity have been much more critical of Islam, than Islam has been of them. This is evidenced by the following quote from the Qu'ran:

> *"O people of the Book! Do ye disapprove of us for no other reason than that we believe in God, and the revelation that hath come to us and that which came before us, and perhaps that most of you are rebellious and disobedient?"* [2]

Muslims are largely tolerant and accepting of other religions, because Muhammad taught that God has sent numerous messengers to mankind in order to teach humanity. In fact, Muslims are even required to accept the prophets from the Jewish and Christian tradition as true and accept their teachings. The tolerance of Islam is also shown by the fact that as the Islamic Empire grew and spread across the Middle-East between the 6th and 7th centuries C.E., newly conquered people were not required to convert to Islam; rather, they were allowed to continue to practice the religion of their choice and only convert if they truly desired to practice Islam. Basically, as long as people showed respect for Islam, that respect was reciprocated.

> *"We believe in God, and the revelation given to us, and to Abraham, Isma'il, Isaac, Jacob, and the Tribes, and that*

---

[2] Al-Maidah 5:59

given to Moses and Jesus, and that was given to all prophets from their Lord: We make no difference between one and another of them: And we bow to God in Islam." [3]

Respecting other religions and their messengers is also important to those on The Path. Respecting another religion does not mean that you have to convert to these other religions or even adopt their teachings, practices, or customs. Respecting other religions merely means recognizing that each religion is trying to accomplish the same thing, which is to develop spiritually fulfilled, loving, and compassionate practitioners in their own unique ways. Therefore, there is no reason for animosity. Also, by at least respecting other religions and being open minded, you can deepen your understanding of God. Because each religion offers its own unique perspective on God, you are bound to find new ideas that resonate you. This is best summed up by the twelfth century Sufi Muslim mystic and philosopher Ibn al-Arabi, who said: *"Do not attach yourself to any particular creed exclusively, so that you may disbelieve all the rest. Otherwise, you will lose much good, nay, you will fail to recognize the real truth of the matter. God, the omnipresent and the omnipotent is not confined to any one creed, for, he says, 'wheresoever you turn, there is the face of Allah'."*

Islam's holy book, *The Qur'an (Koran),* is a collection of the revelations that Muhammad is said to have received via the archangel Gabriel. Muslims believe that the revelations contained within *The Qur'an* were revealed to Muhammad over a period of approximately

---

[3] Al-Baqarah 2:136

22 years (approximately 610 A.D. until his death on June 8, 632 A.D.). *The Qur'an* was mostly written down during Muhammad's lifetime, but the primary transmission of *The Qur'an* was oral, which is where *The Qur'an* gets its name, which literally means "the recitation". The fact that *The Qur'an* was primarily recited orally could explain some of the contradictory passages in *The Qur'an*; however, most of the contradicting passages can be explained by the fact that much of *The Qur'an* is advice on various issues that faced the early Muslim community. The early Muslim community faced a wide range of issues that were constantly evolving over the 22 year period of revelation, so the advice given was often addressed to a specific issue facing the community. For example, Muhammad began preaching his message of monotheism to the people of Mecca, who where polytheists. The people of Mecca rejected his message and even plotted to kill him and his followers, which caused the early Muslim community to eventually flee the area. Therefore, many of the messages that have been used by radical groups to justify violence, were actually written during times when the newly formed Islamic community was literally under attack and fighting for its very existence. During the more stable times, the message of peace, love, unity, co-operation, and the necessity for a deep and personal relationship with God was at the forefront of the revelations.

Islam, like all other Abrahamic religions, is primarily concerned with developing a deeply personal relationship with God through the total submission of yourself to God and his divine will. In fact, "Islam" literally means, "submission". Muslims believe that it is not enough to merely go through the motions of faith and devotion; you must yearn for a deeper relationship with God with every fiber of your being. You must also be willing to actually put God's will into practice and refrain from negative acts. If you fail to act in accordance with the will of God, that constitutes a sin, and you will be held accountable for your sins on the day of judgment. It is important to note that Muslims reject the Christian concept that all humans are somehow born sinful, which is known as the concept of "original sin". Instead, Muslims believe that while we are all born with natural human tendencies, it is our actions and choices that will determine what kind of afterlife we will receive.

> *"… Every soul draws the meed of its acts on none but itself: no bearer of burdens can bear the burden of another. Your goal in the end is towards God: He will tell you the truth of the things which you disputed."* [4]

Muslims adhere to what are known as the "Five Pillars of Faith", which form the foundational requirements of the Islamic faith, and are as follows:

1) *Shahada* – affirmation
2) *Salat* – prayer
3) *Zakat* – alms giving
4) *Siyam* – fasting
5) *Hajj* – pilgrimage

---

[4] Al-An'am 6:164

The Affirmation Pillar (*Shahada*) requires that Muslims believe in only one all-powerful God (Allah), his messengers, and in the Day of Judgment. The Shahada is an affirmation normally recited only in Arabic, *"lâ ilâha illallâh, Muhammadur rasûlullâh"* (There is no god but God, and Muhammad is the Messenger of God). Muslims recite the Shahada in prayer, and people wishing to convert to Islam are required to recite the Shahada. By reciting the Shahada, the Muslim, or the convert, is affirming their belief in the teachings of Muhammad, and is therefore accepting Islam as their faith. This is similar to the Christian belief that one must formally "ask" Jesus to come into their heart in order for them to become a Christian. The recognition that Muhammad was a messenger of God is important to Muslims because this shows respect and admiration towards the founder of the religion.

The affirmation that there is no God but God mirrors the teachings of the other Abrahamic faiths. For example, Maimonides' fifth principle of Jewish faith, that God alone should be the object of worship, especially parallels this pillar. The Affirmation Pillar is important, because it forces Muslims to make God the sole object of their admiration and Worship. Also, since there is only one God, this reinforces that God must have created every human being. Since God created every human being, God loves every human being, and wants us to live in peace and harmony.

> *"O mankind! We created you from a single pair of a male and a female, and made you into nations and tribes, that ye may know each other, not that ye may despise each other.*

Verily the most honored of you in the sight of God is he who is the most righteous of you. And God has full knowledge and is well acquainted with all things." [5]

Unfortunately, too often, people tend to focus on our differences, which only causes division and strife. Those on The Path must take care too focus on those things that unite us, rather than those things that divide us.

The Prayer Pillar (*Salat*) requires that Muslims pray at least 5 times a day while facing the Kabba in Mecca. Muslims traditionally pray at dawn, noon, mid-afternoon, sunset, and at night. The Salat is a ritual prayer that is intended to turn the devotees focus to God alone. It is important to note that although Muslims are required to pray a "ritualized prayer", the practice of prayer is still seen as direct communication with God. The required actions of the Muslim faith, such as prayer, are intended to be a vehicle to receive God's love. Muslims are required to not just merely go through the motions of religious devotions; instead, Muslims are expected to truly experience God's love. The revelations of Muhammad make it clear, much as Jesus did, that merely going through the motions is not enough to please God, and enter into heaven.

"It is not righteousness that you turn your faces to the East and the West; but righteous is he who believes in Allah and the Last Day and the angels and the Scripture and the prophets; and give wealth, for love of Him, to kinsfolk and to orphans and the needy and the wayfarer and to those who

---

[5] Al-Hujurat 49:13

ask, and to set slaves free; and observes proper worship and pay to the poor their due. And those who keep their treaty when they make one, and the patient in tribulation and adversity and time of stress. Such are they who are sincere. Such are the God-fearing." [6]

"O you who believe! seek assistance through patience and prayer; surely Allah is with the patient." [7]

By praying to God throughout the day in order to thank him for their many blessings, the Muslim's mind is being constantly refocused on God. Similarly, other religions use this technique by having devotees recite a mantra, a prayer, or undergo specific types of meditational practices throughout the day.

The practice of continual reflection is something that should be practiced by all people on The Path towards spiritual development. By simply focusing your mind on God throughout the day, you will make yourself more aware of God's many gifts and blessings. The practice of prayer can be a quick and simple acknowledgment of the numerous blessings that surround you, or it can be a more elaborate "conversation" with God. It is important during these times of communion that you focus on your many gifts and blessings rather than only focusing on what you desire. Focusing on the positive aspects of life also has the benefit of making you a more positive person, because your focus will be drawn away from negative aspects. After all, there is no point or benefit gained by focusing on the negative aspects

---

[6] Al-Baqarah 2:177
[7] Al-Baqarah 2:153

of your life, because every bump in the road of life is only temporary. All things no matter how bad they seem will eventually pass. Even if the bump in the road involves death, it too will pass, because after death you will simply move onto the next stage of existence.

The Alms Giving (*Zakat*) Pillar requires that Muslims give a portion of their income to help the poor and needy, as well as to help the spread of Islam. The Zakat is mandatory for all Muslims who can afford it, and in some predominately Islamic countries, a tax is enforced for this purpose. The amount of the Zakat varies, but usually the amount is approximately 2.5% of the total income or assets that have been held for more than a year. The belief in giving alms is derived from the fact that since God has created everything, everything ultimately belongs God. Therefore, by giving support to those less fortunate than yourself, you are merely redistributing the gifts of God. For those on The Path, giving up something that you possess, whether it be time or material wealth, to those less fortunate will help you to better appreciate your blessings, not to mention the positive impact on the life of someone else. It is important to note that when you practice charity, it should not be in order to bring yourself honor or to show just how pious and faithful you are, because this makes a fool out of you and humiliates the person receiving the charity. When you make a show out of charity, you are in essence attempting to put yourself above the receiver, which means you believe that you are somehow better than they are. Instead, give charity out of love and compassion. Make sure that you have only pure intentions in mind and that the receiver is not embarrassed or degraded in any way.

"If you give alms openly, it is well, and if you hide it and give it to the poor, it is better for you; and this will do away with some of your evil deeds; and Allah is aware of what you do." [8]

The Fasting Pillar (*Siyam*) requires that Muslims observe fasting during the month of Ramadan. Ramadan is said to be the month in which Muhammad received his first revelation. During the Islamic month of Ramadan, Muslims who are physically able, should not eat, drink, or have sexual relations from sunrise to sunset. During this time Muslims are supposed to express their gratitude to God, atone for their sins, and think of the poor and destitute. The fasting during this month is designed to encourage a feeling of thankfulness and closeness to God. By depriving yourself of your bodily needs, it helps you appreciate your many gifts, because you can relate to those who are less fortunate than yourself, especially those who have to endure perpetual hunger and thirst. By also overcoming your cravings for nourishment, although temporarily since you are permitted to eat when the sun is at rest, you are overcoming your physical desires in order to pursue spiritual matters.

"O ye who believe! Fasting is prescribed to you as it was prescribed to those before you, that ye may learn self-restraint (God-Consciousness)." [9]

"Ramadhan is the month in which was sent down the Qur'an, as a guide to mankind, also clear signs for guidance and judgment between right and wrong. So every one of you

---

[8] Al-Baqarah 2:271
[9] Al-Baqarah 2:183

who is present at his home during that month should spend it in fasting, but if any one is ill, or on a journey, the prescribed period Should be made up later. God intends every facility for you; He does not want to put to difficulties. He wants you to complete the prescribed period, and to glorify Him in that He has guided you; and perchance you shall be grateful." [10]

Fasting has been practiced by almost every culture in some form or another. The Native Americans (both in North America and South America) would practice rites of fasting in order to end a famine, prevent disease, or simply appease to God. Many Jews practice fasting on several holidays, including Yom Kippur, which serves as a form of penance and to spiritually cleanse themselves for the next year. Many Christians also practice fasting as a form of penance, and in preparation for certain religious events, especially in the Catholic Church. Even the Buddha is said to have undertaken a period of asceticism prior to his enlightenment. Those on The Path can fast as a way to overcome their desires, as well as focus their attention on God and the many blessings that he has provided for them.

The Pilgrimage Pillar (*Hajj*) requires every Muslim who is able to travel to Mecca and observe the Hajj at least once during their lifetime. The Hajj is a pilgrimage taken during the Islamic month of Dhu al-Hijjah. During the Hajj the pilgrim will dress in two seamless white sheets, which shows purity, piety, and unity with the other pilgrims on the Hajj. This is accomplished, because class distinction

---

[10] Al-Baqarah 2:185

and any sense of fashion disappears when the outward trappings of expensive (or inexpensive) clothing are removed. The Hajj is also an important symbol of peace and unity, because during the Hajj race, nationality, and social classes disappear, and all the focus is placed on God. Each pilgrim knows that they are all there for the same reason, and that is to personally experience God in the holiest place on earth for Muslims.

During the Hajj the pilgrims will conduct several rituals including: walking around a structure known as the Kabbah seven times counterclockwise, kissing the black stone in the corner of the Kabbah (if possible), symbolically stoning the Devil, and finally, shaving their heads, which represents a fresh start. The Hajj is an important spiritual pilgrimage for Muslims, because it is a quest to go to the holiest place on earth for Muslims. For Muslims, Mecca is so holy that every Muslim is required to pray towards it when they are giving their daily prayers (Salat). Therefore, for Muslims to actually visit this holy place and take part in the age-old rituals is truly a holy and life-changing event. The concept of a spiritual quest is important, because it allows you to take a spiritual journey while remaining in the physical world. Spiritual quests also allow you to experience God in a real way that can be shared and co-experienced with other people.

Islam's overall message of total submission to God is important to those on The Path, because by totaling submitting yourself to God, you will be putting yourself in the best possible position to truly experience a real relationship with God. Through complete submission, you will gain a better understanding and appreciation of the many gifts and blessings that God has provided for you. Finally, by combining submission to God with an understanding of Divine Truth, you will begin to realize that we are all part of God's creation, which makes us all equal in God's eyes. Hopefully, humanity as a whole will one day realize this sublimely simple and profound truth, and stop persecuting and killing each other over misunderstandings, ignorance, and simple turf wars.

> *"And the Jews say the Christians follow nothing true, and the Christians say the Jews follow nothing true; yet both are readers of the Scripture. Even thus speak those who know not. Allah will judge between them on the Day of Resurrection concerning that wherein they differ."* [11]

> *"O People of the Book! come to common terms as between us and you: That we worship none but God; that we associate no partners with him; that we erect not, from among ourselves, Lords and patrons other than God. If then they turn back, say to them: 'Bear witness that we at least are Muslims (bowing to God's Will)'."* [12]

---

[11] Al-Baqarah 2:113
[12] Aal-Imran 3:64

HINDUISM

Hinduism, with its roots dating back at least to the Iron Age, is believed to be the world's oldest continuously practiced religion. Hinduism is currently the third most practiced religion in the world (Christianity being the first, and Islam being the second). One way that Hinduism differs from the Abrahamic religions is that it does not have a central historical human figure that is credited with founding the religion. Instead, Hinduism is based off of the Vedic traditions and is sometimes called *Sanātana Dharma* (a Sanskrit phrase meaning "the eternal law"). The term "Hindu" comes from the Sanskrit word *"Sindhu"*, which was a term for the people living in the Indus River region that is now part of Northwestern India. Therefore, originally the term Hindu was a name simply used to describe the population of people living in the India subcontinent and was not used as a term for any particular religion. There are many diverse and complex religious beliefs in Hinduism, and the concept of calling the various belief systems based around Vedic traditions, "Hinduism", only began in the 18th century when Europeans began referring to those who practiced the ancient Vedic based religions of India as "Hindus".

For the purposes of this book, the general concepts of Hinduism will be explored, along with the four principle yoga paths.

Unlike the Abrahamic religions that generally have a single authoritative sacred text, Hinduism has numerous sacred texts. The oldest texts, *The Vedas* (written in approximately 1500 B.C.) are considered to be the most important and are the foundation of any religion or sect associated with Hinduism, which is where the term "Vedic religion" comes from. Other important Hindu texts include *The Upanishads*, *The Mahabharata*, *The Ramayana*, *The Brahmanas*, *The Sutrus*, and *The Aranyakas*. All of these sacred texts contain the poems, stories, rituals, and philosophies that the various Hindu sects draw their beliefs from.

When many people think of a polytheistic faith, they immediately think of Hinduism. While Hindus believe in many Gods, they actually believe in one all-powerful force called Brahman (the ultimate form of God), which represents the eternal, infinite, and unchanging reality from which all of creation is manifested, including spiritual beings.

> *"He is the one God, hidden in all beings, all-pervading, the*
> *Self within all beings, watching over all works, dwelling in*
> *all beings, the witness, the perceiver, the only one, free from*
> *qualities".* [1]

The numerous "sub-deities" (spiritual beings) in the Hindu Pantheon are merely manifestations of Brahman. The sub-deities are

---

[1] Svetasvatara Upanishad 6.11

created from God, just as we are all created from God, and are on earth to help guide different aspects of creation. The benevolent sub-deities are known as "*Devas*", while the malevolent beings are known as "*Asuras*". The deities in the Hindu Pantheon are believed to have numerous powers that represent the different aspects of God. Since these various sub-deities possess different characteristics and powers, Hindus can worship or pray to a particular deity in order to receive help that falls within that deities power, much like the angels, prophets, and saints in the Abrahamic faiths.

In Hinduism the ultimate, all-powerful, and largely unknowable form of God is characterized by what is known as the Brahman Trinity, which is composed of the three principle deities: Brahma, Vishnu, and Shiva. The concept of the Brahman Trinity closely mirrors the Christian Trinity in that there is an all-powerful God that is manifested in three different ways. In the Brahman Trinity there is the "Creator" known as Brahma, the "Preserver" known as Vishnu, and the "Destroyer" known as Shiva. This principle Trinity of Hinduism is made up of three distinct incarnations of Brahman, yet all of the incarnations are still Brahman. This is similar to Christianity, where there is a Trinity composed of "God the Father", "Jesus the Son", and the "Holy Ghost". Hinduism, like Christianity, believes that all manifestations of the Trinity are all part of God, yet each serves a distinct purpose and role in creation, and in the life cycle of the universe.

"Just as light is diffused from a fire which is confined to one spot, so is this whole universe the diffused energy of the supreme Brahman. And as light shows a difference, greater or less, according to its nearness or distance from the fire, so is there a variation in the energy of the impersonal Brahman. Brahma, Vishnu, and Shiva are his chief energies". [2]

As is illustrated by the Brahman Trinity, there are creative and destructive forces, and good and evil (positive and negative) forces in the universe that both oppose and compliment each other, which keeps the universe balanced. Just as there is light in the world, there is also darkness. Both are essential, because without darkness, one would not be able to understand or appreciate light. In the same way, without evil in the world, one would not be able to understand and appreciate goodness. In many ways the universe is in the midst of a constant balancing act between the positive and negative forces. When the forces are balanced, there is order; when the forces are unbalanced, there is chaos. Just as a magnet is composed of opposite poles that can be used to repel one another, they can also be used to create an almost inseparable bond. It is the space between the positive and negative forces where the ultimate form of God resides and where the true seeker along The Path seeks to reside as well.

"These two paths, the light and the dark, are said to be eternal, lending some to liberation and others to rebirth. Once you have known these two paths, Arjuna, you can never be deluded again. Attain this knowledge through per-

---

[2] Vishnu Purana 1

severance in yoga. There is merit in studying the scriptures, in selfless service, austerity, and giving, but the practice of meditation carries you beyond all these to the supreme abode of the highest Lord." [3]

In Hinduism and many of the western mystery traditions, there is the belief that the further we separate ourselves from God, the more negative energy we will be exposed to. This is based on the belief that the pure loving creative force of God (light) is diluted as we become separated from the ultimate form of God, which is evidenced by the numerous stories involving the "fall of man". The material world that we exist in acts as a veil that scatters the light of God, thus allowing negative energies, and even evil, to exist, whereas they cannot exist in higher spiritual realms, because the light of God is too strong. This concept can be visualized by passing pure light through a prism, which then separates the light into various colors. God would represent the initial pure white light, while the light that has passed through the prism (the material world) has become diluted, which allows less pure things, like evil, to exist. However, with additional work, and the proper instruments, this diluted light can become reconstituted into pure light once again. The goal of The Path is to pierce the veil of material existence in order to reconnect with the pure light of God, which in Hinduism is accomplished through the yogic paths that will be discussed shortly.

This visualization of reconstituting diluted light is useful for people on The Path. Many mystery schools in both the East and

---

[3] Bhagavad-Gita 8:26-28

West, teach that God is pure light (pure energy) and that humanity is living in a world of diluted light. Therefore, the journey of spiritual development can be visualized as leaving the world of darkness, in order to reconnect with the pure light of God. This visualization can also be a powerful visualization tool during meditation. During meditation, try to visualize (imagine) your true-self, the divine spark from God, as a point of energy (light) in your mind's eye. As you begin the meditation, imagine the light as dim, hazy, or even discolored, because it is being clouded by your negative thoughts and emotions. As you begin to examine and strip away your negative thoughts and emotions, imagine the light getting brighter and purer, until you are surrounded by the pure light of your divine spark, stay in this pure space and let its energy recharge you before ending the session and returning to the material world. Use this technique as necessary to overcome times when you are depressed, or feeling negative.

The concept of *Karma* is central to Hindu thought and should be familiar to many Westerners thanks to many familiar sayings and references in popular culture. *Karma* is basically a spiritual law of cause and effect. *Karma* is a spiritual force that, based on our past actions, helps to shape what will happen to us in the future. If we do good deeds and actions then we will receive positive *Karma*, which means that good things will generally happen to us. If we do bad things, then we will receive negative *Karma* and bad things will generally happen to us. Basically, *Karma* is what allows us to reap what we sow. If we live a good life, good things will happen to us, and if we live a bad life, we will suffer the consequences. The concept of

Karma is easy to see at work in every day life, in that people who help others and do what is right generally live happy and fulfilled lives, while people who do bad deeds and undertake destructive behaviors lead brutish lives filled with disappointment. It is important to note that Hindus also believe that the law of *Karma* does not end when we die, because our *Karma* will follow us into the next stage of life. Therefore, Hindus believe that we must do good things in this life or we may suffer in the next life, and suffering from this life may be caused by bad *Karma* from our previous lives.

The concept of *Karma* is important to those on The Path, because it helps to reinforce that our actions and our intentions are important. If we purposefully and needlessly harm or take advantage of our environment, animals, or especially other people, then we deserve to suffer the consequences of our actions. Therefore, it is important to help our fellow man, as well as help creation as a whole, because what we put out into the world is what we will receive back. In the same way, what we put into our spiritual journey is what we will get back. Hindus believe that *Karma* is also affected by what our intentions behind our actions are; therefore, if we "do" a lot of good things but do not have pure intentions (we want praise, or some sort of social advancement), then negative *Karma* may still result.

> *"In order to achieve good result, a pious-objective is determined first and then followed by good Karma for its accomplishment."* [4]

---

[4] Rig-Veda 31/14

Another important aspect of the Hindu religion is the concept of reincarnation. The concept of reincarnation is that after death, the souls of creatures are reborn into a new body. Whether you are reincarnated in a human or an animal body will depend on your *Karma* at the time of your death. If you have lived a good life and have done good things (yet have not reached *Moksha*), you will likely be reincarnated once again as a human and, according to some traditions, into a higher social class. If you have lived a bad life, some traditions say that you will be born into a lesser form, such as some sort of animal, or into a low social class. The concept of reincarnation mirrors most of the world religions in that after death our souls will take on a new form in either a pleasurable existence (heaven) or in an existence full of suffering (hell). In many ways the concept of reincarnation also mirrors the laws of physics. In the physical world the concept of reincarnation can be viewed as a droplet of water as it undergoes the hydrologic cycle. During the hydrologic cycle, the water droplet may begin its lifecycle as a droplet of water, which then becomes frozen in a block of ice. Later, it turns into a molecule of gas that finally reforms as a droplet of water in a cloud to begin the cycle once more. During the many stages of the water droplet's physical life, it still contains its basic molecular make up. It is still water, no matter what physical stage it is in. In the same way, Hindus believe that the soul may be reincarnated many times, yet it still retains its unique character.

As in all the religions that teach Truth, the goal of Hinduism is to help its adherents to transcend this current world in order to reunite with God so that they can experience God's bliss and love in this lifetime, as well as after death. In Hinduism the goal is to reach *Moksha*, which literally means "release". As mentioned, Hindus believe in reincarnation and that this world is full of pain and suffering; therefore, to be constantly born over and over again in this world, a cycle called *Samsara*, has inherent suffering. When someone reaches *Moksha* they are released from the pain and suffering of *Samsara*. In order to achieve *Moksha* the individual must reach *Atma-Jnana* (self-realization). Self-realization occurs when you realize that your true-self, called the Atman, is really intertwined with all of creation and therefore with God. While the Atman composes your true-self and is therefore inherently unique to you, it is your ego that leads you to believe that "you" are somehow separate and apart from all of creation. It is the ego's need to feel special, unique, and self-important which prevents self-realization and ultimately *Moksha* to occur.

> *"The person whose mind is always free from attachment,*
> *who has subdued the mind and senses, and who is free*
> *from desires, attains the supreme perfection of freedom from*
> *Karma through renunciation".* [5]

In order to facilitate self-realization and ultimately *Moksha*, Hinduism has four principle paths (Yogas): *Jnana Yoga* (Thinking), *Bhakti Yoga* (Devotion), *Karma Yoga* (Action), and *Raja Yoga* (Meditation).

---

[5] Bhagavad-Gita 18.49

Jnana Yoga is known as the way of knowledge and has traditionally been used by people who are inclined towards intellectual pursuits. This path is considered the shortest and most difficult path towards achieving *Moksha*. The goal of *Jnana Yoga* is to have the adherent overcome the three impurities of human existence: egoism, desire, and the illusion that we are separate from God and all of creation. *Jnana Yoga* focuses on the ultimate reality of God rather than a more personal form of God. *Jnana Yoga* focuses on learning to control your senses, mind, and very thoughts in such a way that will allow you to awaken your true-self, which has been always been connected with God yet hindered by the ego. According to *Jnana Yoga*, in order to obtain true knowledge you must: 1) become educated in the study of scriptures; 2) purify the mind and body through self discipline; 3) become aware of the true nature of the world and yourself by practicing disciplines such as meditation that will then allow you to deeply reflect and concentrate on Divine Truth, which will allow you to reach self-realization. This path is considered to be the most difficult path, because in order to undertake this path, you must delve into the inner-most realms of your psyche in order to purify and perfect yourself until self-realization is obtained.

> *"Contemplating and meditating on the 'real-self' accelerates this process of self-development and makes liberation possible".* [6]

---

[6] Atharva-Veda 34/3

Reaching self-realization requires that you realize that the real "you" is not your body. The real you is the "knower", the soul that was created by God and seeks to reunite with God. Therefore, you must learn to let go of your ego, your painful experiences, your self-doubt, etc. and learn to love yourself, all of creation, and ultimately God unconditionally. In order to accomplish this you must learn to not focus on the negative and material aspects that create perceived separation between yourself and God.

> *"Those who see with eyes of knowledge the difference between the body and the knower of the body, and can also understand the process of liberation from bondage in material nature, attain to the supreme goal".* [7]

Bhakti Yoga, the path of devotion, is the most widely practiced form of yoga. The goal of *Bhakti Yoga* is to foster a personal relationship with a personal form of God, such as a one of the Devas. According to *The Bhagavata Purana* there are nine devotions which the adherent should follow: 1) listening to the scriptures; 2) praising God; 3) remembering God daily; 4) render service to God; 5) worship an image or representation of God; 6) pay homage to God; 7) servitude; 8) friendship; and 9) complete surrender of the self. This form of yoga closely mirrors the concept of religion that many Westerners follow in that God is viewed as a personal being, which can be directly accessed. In fact, this form of yoga can be seen in most Christian church services where the congregation listens to

---

[7] Bhagavad-Gita 13.35

pre-selected scriptures which are read, songs to God/Jesus are sung, a cross or picture of Jesus is hung prominently in the sanctuary, offerings are taken, and usually several prayers of thanks and surrender are given. This path is useful in that it is a much more public path than *Jnana Yoga*, which allows the practitioner to build a support group of fellow practitioners around themselves that will help guide them along their path. Also, by focusing your devotions on a personal form of God, it is easier to feel connected to God, which may allow you to remain more engaged on your spiritual path and development.

> *"Engage your mind always in thinking of Me, become My devotee, offer obeisances to Me and worship Me. Being completely absorbed in Me, surely you will come to Me"* [8].

> *"One can understand Me as I am, as the supreme personality of the Godhead, only by devotional service. And when one is in full consciousness of Me by such devotion, he can enter into the kingdom of God".* [9]

Karma Yoga, discipline of action, is principally concerned with correct action and is based on the teachings contained in the famous *Bhagavad Gita*, which is part of the *Mahabharata*. The goal of *Karma Yoga* is to change your thoughts, actions, and desires to such an extent that they naturally align with God's will, thus allowing self-realization and *Moksha* to occur. In order to follow along this path, you must give selfless service to humanity and God's creation as a whole. This means that you must remove your attachment to the physical

---

[8] Bhagavad-Gita 9.34
[9] Bhagavad-Gita 18.55

world and do good deeds, without seeking any kind of reward or praise, which only serves to feed the ego.

> *"Therefore, without being attached to the fruits of activities, one should act as a matter of duty, for by working without attachment one attains the Supreme Goal".* [10]

By selflessly helping God's creation you will be acting in concert with what God is constantly doing. Also, by helping humanity and God's creation as a whole, you will be acting like a lighthouse that reflects God's love out into a world of darkness, which is in need of your help.

Finally, *Raja Yoga*, the royal yoga, is principally concerned with reaching self-realization through meditation. By calming the mind and focusing on God through meditation you will be able to clear the mental clutter that prevents you from directly experiencing God. Everyone has mental clutter that includes things like: worries about your job, family, money, and friendships, feelings of guilt or regret from your past, feelings of doubt, etc. Most of this mental clutter is created by the ego, which seeks to remain in control by causing confusion and mental clutter.

> *"All minds are created by ego-the separate sense of 'I.' All these expressions of individuality, however highly developed, are the impulses of the force of evolution. And of these, only the mind born of meditation is free from the latent impressions that generated desire".* [11]

---

[10] Bhagavad-Gita 3.19
[11] The Yoga Sutras of Patanjali, 4:4-6

Raja Yoga traditionally has eight different aspects which the adherent should follow:

1) *Yama* – self-restraint
2) *Niyama* – religious observance
3) *Asana* – integration of the mind and body through physical activity
4) *Pranayama* – integration of the mind and body through the regulation of your breath
5) *Pratyahara* – withdrawal of senses
6) *Dharana* – concentration of the mind
7) *Dhyana* – quiet meditation
8) *Samadhi* – state of blissful awareness

By practicing *Raja Yoga,* your life becomes a kind of living meditation, where you are constantly focusing on your connection with God during every moment of your life through your physical and mental activities, even the control of your breath.

"With senses and mind constantly controlled through meditation, united with the Self within, an aspirant attains nirvana, the state of abiding joy and peace in me". [12]

The four different types of traditional Hindu yogas allow a seeker on the path towards spiritual development to pick a type of religious practice that bests suits them. After all, a spiritual path should not be, and is not, a one size fits all program. A spiritual path is something that is deeply personal, and what works for someone, might not necessarily work for others or yourself. Also, the four types of

---

[12] Bhagavad-Gita 6.15

yoga closely mirror personal development and religious experiences that most people have, no matter what religion they associate with. For example, when someone begins their path they may be attracted to more of a *Bhakti* type of yoga, where they have a structured religious experience around a very personal God. After awhile, a person may become drawn to a type of *Karma Yoga* where they feel the need to help people through volunteer projects and charities. Eventually, a person may become drawn to a type of *Raja Yoga* where they integrate their religious experience into every aspect of their life. Finally, a person may be drawn to *Jnana Yoga* where they begin to delve inside of themselves in order to reach a form of direct communion with the ultimate form of God by melding their own personal psyche with God's ever-present reality and love. Therefore, do not be afraid to try or borrow from a different spiritual practice if it will help you along your own spiritual path.

Hinduism is an important religion because it not only set the foundation for many of the Eastern religions, especially Buddhism, but it arguably influenced, in one form or another, many of the other religions of the world. Furthermore, Hinduism teaches that every human being and all of creation is intimately connected to God, because God is the force that created and continues to create everything in the universe. However, on an ultimate level God is simply a creative force that can neither be angered nor persuaded to give a particular favor. God is simply love. The four yoga paths provide different ways to connect with God through religious devotions, daily actions, meditations, and finally your very thoughts. By shaping our devotions, actions, meditations, and thoughts to solely reflect the love of God, we will not only change our inner thoughts to become more tuned into God, which allows us to experience a blissful state in this life and in the next, but we will reflect the love of God out into the world, which will make the world a better place long after this life has ended.

> *"The person who treads on the path of truth and his mind free from negative qualities like fear, wickedness and with the desire of benefit of all, is long lived".* [13]

---

[13] Rig-Veda 3/1 83

BUDDHISM

Buddhism is currently estimated to be the fourth largest religion in the world, with approximately 375 million followers. Buddhism grew out of the teachings of Siddhartha Gautama, which many people know simply as "the Buddha". The Buddha lived and taught in what is now northeastern India sometime between the 4th and 6th Century B.C.E. There are various branches and sects that have developed out of the Buddha's teachings. The three major branches of Buddhism are:

1) *Theravada Buddhism* (Way of the Elders) is the oldest existing and most conservative branch of Buddhism, which is most prevalent in Southeast Asia
2) *Mahayana Buddhism* (The Great Vehicle) is currently the most practiced branch and includes the Zen Buddhist schools
3) *Vajrayana* (The Diamond Vehicle) composes the more esoteric and tantric schools of Buddhism, such as Tibetan Buddhism

Like Jesus and Muhammad later, the Buddha was not seeking to begin or teach a new religion, he was merely teaching Divine Truth. Also, like Muhammad, the Buddha never claimed to be God;

he only claimed to be an awakened teacher. In fact, in a famous exchange he was directly asked whether or not he was a god, and his response was simply "no". He was then asked what exactly he was, to which he simply replied "I am awake".

The teachings of the Buddha are known as *Buddha-Dharma* (Buddha teachings), and each branch of Buddhism has its own holy books based on the teachings of the Buddha. *Theravada Buddhism* recognizes *The Tripitaka* (aka *Pali Canon*), *Mahayana Buddhism* recognizes the Chinese *Tripitaka* and various *Sutras*, and *Tibetan Buddhism* recognizes *The Kangyur* and *Tengyur*. For the purposes of this book, only the fundamental teachings of the Buddha will be explored, which are the Four Noble Truths, the Eightfold Path, and the Three Jewels.

According to Buddhist tradition, the Buddha, known as Siddhartha Gautama prior to his enlightenment, was born a prince. One day a sage prophesized to his father that Siddhartha would become a great warrior king; however, if he were ever exposed to suffering, he would become a master of the spiritual path and a great teacher. His father was horrified at the thought of his son becoming a spiritual teacher, because he wanted his son to be a great warrior king, just as he had been. Therefore, his father confined young Siddhartha to the palace grounds and gave him every luxury and pleasure possible in an attempt to make sure that he was never exposed to any form of suffering or pain. During this time, young Siddhartha became well educated in the arts, sciences, and philosophies of the time, especially the Vedic (Hindu) traditions.

Eventually, Siddhartha did come into contact with human suffering in what are known as "The Four Encounters". It is said that while riding in his chariot Siddhartha was exposed to suffering in the forms of old age, disease, and death by coming into contact with an old man, a sick man, and a funeral procession. (Some versions say that he viewed these from his palace walls.) Siddhartha was distraught by his first glimpses of human suffering, and suffering began to consume his thoughts. However, his fourth encounter was with an ascetic beggar/monk who told Siddhartha that undertaking the spiritual path would alleviate his suffering. Soon after his four encounters, as he was nearing the time of his coronation, Siddhartha and his wife had a child; however, his desire to pursue the spiritual path continued to grow. Eventually, Siddhartha made the heart wrenching decision to leave his wife, child, and life of luxury behind in order to enter a monastery and become a monk.

After several years as a monk, Siddhartha failed to reach an enlightened state; therefore, he left the monastery in order to travel and learn deeper spiritual teachings. During Siddhartha's travels he learned how to enter into deep states of meditations (*Samadhi*). After failing to reach pure enlightenment through Samadhi alone, Siddhartha joined a group of ascetics and began an extensive period of asceticism where he would only allow himself to eat a few grains of rice a day while maintaining a constant state of meditation. After six years of asceticism, Siddhartha was near death from malnutrition when he came to the realization that asceticism alone would not allow him to reach pure enlightenment. Siddhartha realized for the first time that neither extreme of luxury nor extreme asceticism would allow him to reach true enlightenment. Instead, he realized that he must find the "middle way". Much to the dismay of his ascetic companions, Siddhartha discontinued his extreme ascetic practices and was nursed back to health by a young woman.

According to Buddhist tradition, after regaining his health, Siddhartha took a pile of kusha grass, spread it under a bodhi tree, and entered into a deep *Samadhi* during the night. During his *Samadhi*, Siddhartha entered into several spiritual realms, until he was finally challenged by a powerful demon, Mara. Mara first tried to tempt Siddhartha to break his meditation by offering Siddhartha his three beautiful daughters, which failed. Mara then sent an army of demons to attack Siddhartha, which also failed. Finally, Mara tried to directly attack Siddhartha, yet still Siddhartha maintained his meditation. At the end of the night, Siddhartha became fully enlightened and learned how to end the suffering of all sentient beings. From that day forward Siddhartha Gautama became simply known as "the Buddha" ("the awakened one" or the "enlightened one"), and he dedicated the rest of his life to ending the suffering of all sentient beings. The temptation of Siddhartha during this meditation period mirrors the later biblical narrative of how Jesus Christ was tempted by Satan after experiencing an extended period of fasting and prayer (meditation) for 40 days and 40 nights.

The teachings of Buddhism, no matter the sect, are primarily concerned with ending the suffering of sentient beings as quickly as possible. In order to end suffering, it is essential for the individual to become "awakened", which is essentially a peaceful and blissful state of fulfillment, harmony, and awareness (self-actualization). Becoming awakened means to realize your ultimate nature, which is interconnected with everything in the universe, including every living being and ultimately "God". Once you realize your interconnectedness with all of creation, it is natural to try and end the suffering of not only yourself, but each living being, which is why the Buddha taught that one should not seek enlightenment for personal gain alone. Instead, you should seek enlightenment in order to end the suffering of others and perform acts of compassion, understanding, tolerance, and ultimately love, which will also facilitate happiness and awakening within yourself and others. According to H.H. the 14th Dalai Lama- Tenzin Gyatso:

> *"I believe that the very purpose of life is to be happy. From the very core of our being, we desire contentment. In my own limited experience I have found that the more we care for the happiness of others, the greater is our own sense of well-being. Cultivating a close, warmhearted feeling for others automatically puts the mind at ease. It helps remove whatever fears or insecurities we may have and gives us the strength to cope with any obstacles we encounter. It is the principal source of success in life. Since we are not solely material creatures, it is a mistake to place all our hopes for happiness on external development alone. The key is to develop inner peace."*

In order to end the suffering of sentient beings, the Buddha taught what are known as the Four Noble Truths, and these teachings form the foundation of all Buddhist beliefs. The Four Noble Truths are as follows:

1) *Dukkha* – truth of suffering
2) *Samudaya* – truth of the cause of suffering
3) *Nirhodha* – truth of the end of suffering
4) *Magga* – truth of the path which leads to the cessation of suffering

The fact that Buddhism spends so much time focusing on suffering does not make it a negative religion, as some people believe. To the contrary, Buddhism focuses on the suffering of sentient beings, so that all suffering can cease. Only by understanding the causes and remedies of suffering and working to end suffering can one begin to truly experience compassion and love, which leads to true peace and the awakening of your true-self. According to the Buddha, *"So awake, reflect, watch. Work with care and attention. Live in the way and the light will grow in you".* [1]

The First Noble Truth, The Truth of Suffering, deals with the fact that the world is full of suffering. Every sentient (living) being suffers in one form or another, whether it is pain, hunger, sickness, injury, old age, depression, disappointment, sadness, fear, frustration, etc. Suffering is the one aspect that unites all living beings, because every living being experiences it. Every person alive is experiencing some sort of suffering, including the person you love the most, the person who made you angry earlier today, and even the person you most despise. If you do not understand and accept that everyone,

---

[1] The Dhammapada Chapter 2

including yourself, suffers you cannot progress spiritually. Taking the time to realize that "you" are not the only living being that suffers is an important step in breaking down the ego, because the ego not only seeks praise, it revels in the suffering of your perceived enemies. The ego also revels in self-suffering. The feeling that "you" are somehow a victim allows you to build an artificial barrier between yourself, the rest of creation, and ultimately God. After you realize that the world is full of suffering, the second step, which is a natural reaction, is to feel compassion and the need to end the suffering of all sentient beings, even our perceived enemies. The realization of universal suffering and the desire to stop the suffering is what led the Buddha to dedicate his life to helping others along the spiritual path. Therefore, those on the spiritual path should not only seek to better themselves, but they should seek to better all sentient beings, because every living thing is intertwined as a creation of God. According to the Buddha:

> *"All beings tremble before violence.*
> *All fear death.*
> *All love life. See yourself in other.*
> *Then whom can you hurt?*
> *What harm can you do?*
> *He who seeks happiness*
> *By hurting those who seek happiness*
> *Will never find happiness.*
> *For your brother is like you.*
> *He wants to be happy.*
> *Never harm him*
> *And when you leave this life*
> *You too will find happiness."* [2]

---

[2] The Dhammapada Chapter 10

The Second Noble Truth, The Truth of the Cause of Suffering, deals with the fact that all suffering is caused by attachment to the impermanent world. The world, our current state of existence, is impermanent because everything is in a constant state of transition. For example: the day is constantly moving towards night, the goals and cravings that you seek, even if satisfied, will disappear into the mist of time, and yourself and your loved ones will all eventually die and move onto the next realm of existence. The attachment to the transitory material world causes suffering, because you will always be suffering either because you are seeking something, or suffering the passing of something. The ego and attachment go hand-in-hand because the ego has a voracious appetite, which is fed by victories and losses alike. The ego loves to cling to things that are transitory, because it can revel in the obtainment of a goal, "I accomplished this", and it can revel in the sorrow when something is lost "I lost this". This does not mean that you shouldn't have feelings and goals, because they are a basic part of being human. The key is to end your attachment to the things that are impermanent, and learn to love life and live in the now. After all, we are not guaranteed how many more moments we will even be alive. According to the Buddha:

> *"You shouldn't chase after the past or place expectations on the future. What is past is left behind. The future is as yet unreached. Whatever quality is present you clearly see right there, right now. Not being taken in, unshaken, that's how you develop the heart. Ardently doing what should be done today, for who knows? You could be dead tomorrow".* [3]

---

[3] The Bhaddekaratta Sutta

The Third Noble Truth, The Truth of the End of Suffering, means that you have the ability to end the cycle of suffering. Buddhists believe that in order to end the continuous cycle of suffering, you must stop craving the things that lead to attachment and clinging. Stopping the cravings that lead to attachment requires you to deeply explore your motivations and thought processes that lead to your cravings to begin with. This does not mean that you will not have any hopes and desires, but you will learn to live fully in the present moment rather than regretting the past or focusing on a future that may never come. You should enjoy life in the same way that you would enjoy a beautiful butterfly that lands on your shoulder; enjoy it and then let it fly away when the time comes. Let life take its natural course. By ending your attachment and suffering, you will be able to find ultimate inner peace and happiness, known as *Nirvana* in Buddhism. According to the Buddha:

> *"From passion and desire,*
> *Sensuousness and lust,*
> *Arise grief and fear.*
> *Free yourself from attachment."* [4]

The Fourth Noble Truth, The Path to the Cessation of Suffering, outlines the gradual path which one must take in order to end suffering. As mentioned, the Buddha realized that he could not reach a state of enlightenment by any extreme path, whether it be extreme luxury, extreme suffering, or even extreme spirituality. Instead, the Buddha realized that the true way to reach enlightenment was to

---

[4] The Dhammapada Chapter 16

find the middle path that balances the various forces and influences of life. The finding and following of a middle path is not unique to Buddhism; in fact, it can even be found visually represented in the Kabbalistic Tree of Life, which contains a path of mercy, a path of severity, and a middle path of ascension. Like Buddhism, Kabbalists believe that one must find balance between the often competing forces of life in order to reach their full spiritual potential.

In order to explain the middle path, the Buddha taught what is known as the Noble Eightfold Path, which the aspirant should undertake in order to reach true enlightenment. This makes up the action part of the Buddhist tradition. It is important to note that Buddhism is much more concerned with the action of eliminating suffering, rather than intellectually discussing how to go about it. The Noble Eightfold Path can be broken down into three sections:

1) "Wisdom" – which is comprised of Right View and Right Intention
2) "Ethical Conduct" – comprised of Right Speech, Right Action, and Right Livelihood
3) "Mental Development" – comprised of Right Effort, Right Mindfulness, and Right Concentration

The eight steps of the Eightfold Path are not intended to be systematic steps; instead, they are to be taken as a whole and used together to aid the practitioner along their path towards personal and spiritual development.

The steps involving "Wisdom" (Right View and Right Intention) involve the cognitive aspects of your mind that lead to true

wisdom. Wisdom does not necessarily have anything to do with intellectual capacity or educational achievement; rather, wisdom means
deeply understanding Truth, which naturally flows from developing
and harnessing your mind. According to the Buddha, *"As the fletcher
whittles and makes straight his arrows, So the master directs his straying
thoughts".* [5] "Right View" deals with understanding the world as it
truly is, which means that you must understand that the world is full
of suffering, the world is impermanent, and that the constant cycle
of suffering that all sentient beings experience must come to an end.
"Right Intention" refers to performing your actions with the correct
mental intention behind them. For example, you shouldn't perform
actions because worldly cravings and desires have influenced you to
do so, or out of anger or passion; instead, you should only intend
to perform actions that will positively affect the world around you,
without seeking material benefits or praise that only feed the ego.

The steps involving "Ethical Conduct" (Right Speech, Right
Action, Right Livelihood), involve performing your actions in ways
that will help to end your own suffering, as well as the suffering of all
sentient beings. For example, we all know that words have power, because they have the ability to create and to destroy. Therefore, "Right
Speech" involves controlling your speech in such a way that it will
only be used for good and never as a weapon. This means not gos-
siping, lying, or speaking badly of another person. "Right Action",
involves controlling your actions so that you will not contribute to

---

[5] The Dhammapada Chapter 3

the suffering of other living beings. Therefore, you should take care not to steal, lie, harm other beings, or engage in sexual misconduct. "Right Livelihood" means not being involved in professions that cause suffering, such as those that harm or kill living beings. By properly channeling and harnessing your conduct you will not only be a happier person, but you will affect the world around you in a positive way. According to the Buddha, *"Speak or act with a pure mind and happiness will follow you as your shadow, unshakable"*. [6]

The steps dealing with "Mental Development" (Right Effort, Right Mindfulness, and Right Concentration), involves training the mind through correct practices to such an extent that doing good deeds and maintaining blissful awareness becomes automatic. "Right Effort" involves controlling the intent of your actions in a manner that will not cause harm or negatively influence other living beings. Instead, you should concentrate your intent on only helping others. "Right Mindfulness" involves not focusing on greed, anxiety, and the material world. Finally, "Right Concentration", involves training your mind to focus on blissful awareness, which aids in the melding of the other eight steps. It is important to note that your mental thoughts are powerful, and uncontrolled or negative thoughts and emotions can harm you, as well as contribute to the suffering of other sentient beings. Therefore, by harnessing your thoughts in a positive and constructive way, you not only help your own spiritual progression, but you will also help others along their own path. According to

---

[6] The Dhammapada Chapter 1

the Buddha, *"Your worst enemy cannot harm you as much as your own thoughts, unguarded. But once mastered, no one can help you as much, not even your father or your mother."* [7]

Finally, Buddhists believe that in order to become a practicing Buddhist you must take refuge in what are known as the "Three Jewels". The Three Jewels are composed of 1) The Buddha – recognizing him as an enlightened being and teacher; 2) The Dharma – recognizing the teachings of the Buddha (called the Buddha Dharma) as a way to achieve enlightenment; and 3) The Sangha – respecting the community of enlightened beings which make up the Buddhist community. Buddhists are encouraged to think for themselves, and to not merely rely on tradition for spiritual development. By thinking for himself/herself, the Buddhist is taking an active role in their own spiritual development, rather than a passive role based on blind obedience. According to the Buddha:

> *"Do not rely upon what has been acquired by repeated tradition; nor upon lineage; nor upon rumor; nor upon what is handed down in the teachings; nor upon logic; nor upon inference; nor upon a consideration of reasons; nor upon a delight in speculation; nor upon appearances; nor upon respect for your teacher. Kalmas, when you know for yourselves: These things are unskillful; these things are blamable; these things are censured by the wise; undertaken and observed, these things lead to harm and suffering, then abandon them."* [8]

---

[7] The Dhammapada Chapter 3
[8] The Kalama Sutta

In conclusion, Buddhism's primary focus of ending the suffering of all sentient beings should powerfully resonate with those on The Path, especially since the motivation to end some kind of personal suffering is generally the motivation that inspires most spiritual seekers to begin their journey in the first place. By understanding universal suffering and following the teachings contained in the Four Noble Truths and the Eightfold Path, you can begin to actually overcome your own suffering, which will then allow you to take steps to end the suffering of others. The goal of undertaking personal and spiritual development in order to ultimately help others is reflected by every religion, because developing inner peace and happiness is useless if the world around you is suffering. Therefore, learn to develop an inner sense of peace, compassion, and loving kindness, and most importantly reflect those attributes into the world.

> *"Let your love flow outward through the universe,*
> *To its height, its depth, its broad extent,*
> *A limitless love, without hatred or enmity.*
> *Then as you stand or walk,*
> *Sit or lie down,*
> *As long as you are awake,*
> *Strive for this with a one-pointed mind;*
> *Your life will bring heaven to earth".* [9]

---

[9] The Kalama Sutta Sutta Nipata

TAOISM

Taoism (pronounced "Dow-ism"), which means "The Path" or "The Way", is a religion purportedly created by a Chinese teacher and philosopher named Lao-Tzu sometime between the seventh and fourth centuries BCE. Lao-Tzu is said to have written the *Tao Te Ching* (The Doctrine of the Way), which is the foundational text for Taoism. Other important texts in Taoism include the *Zhuangzi* and the *Daozang*. Taoism is most prevalent in China and in Asian countries where aspects of Chinese culture are present. The exact number of adherents to Taoism is difficult to calculate, because even though Taoism is an officially sanctioned religion under the Communist Chinese government, the exact figures for practitioners in China are unavailable. Also, many practitioners of Taoism incorporate various aspects of Taoism with other faiths, especially traditional folk religions and Buddhism, so many do not necessarily consider themselves to be strictly Taoists. Nevertheless, most estimates place the number of Taoists at approximately 225 million, which would place it just behind Buddhism in popularity.

According to legend, Lao Tzu was immaculately conceived

when a shooting star entered his mother's (Mother Li's) womb. It is said that Lao Tzu stayed in Mother Li's womb for 62 years until being born after she leaned against a plum tree. Because of his extended gestational period he was born an elderly man with long white hair and a long white beard, which are traditional signs of wisdom in Chinese culture. He is said to have worked as a scholar and records keeper for the Zhou Dynasty, which gave him access to a vast collection of literary and scholarly works. It is said that while he never opened a formal school, Lao Tzu's wisdom was such that he had many followers and disciples. Upon retirement, Lao Tzu intended to ride an ox out of China in order to travel to distant lands in the west; however, his fame and wisdom was such that a guard pleaded with him to write down all of his knowledge before leaving, so that it could be preserved and shared with future generations. Lao Tzu complied, and legend says that his brief written work became the *Tao Te Ching*. After completing the *Tao Te Ching*, Lao Tzu is said to have ridden his ox to distant western lands, where some legends say he influenced numerous spiritual traditions.

Many scholars and practitioners debate whether or not Lao Tzu actually existed. Many believe that it is more likely that Lao Tzu is a mythical archetypal figure and that the *Tao Te Ching* was actually written by several philosophers and teachers. However, like many mythical religious founders, it is really not important if Lao Tzu actually physically existed or not. What is important is the teachings and wisdom contained in the religion that has positively impacted the lives of countless practitioners for over two and a half millennia.

Taoism has existed for over two millennia because its powerful message of balance and harmony has resonated with people throughout the ages and continues to resonate, perhaps more than ever, in today's hectic and chaotic world.

The three main branches of Taoism are: Philosophical Taoism (*Daojia*), Religious Taoism (*Daojiao*), and Folk Taoism (comprised of various aspects from Chinese folk religions). Each branch also contains various sects. The various branches and sects of Taoism can make it difficult to define Taoism, because each branch and sect has its own viewpoints on the religious nature of Taoism, the role of spiritual beings, as well as what spiritual practices are necessary. Some practitioners view Taoism as a true religion. Others view it as more of a philosophy and way of life, rather than as a religion, which makes sense because Taoism originally began as a system of philosophy and did not develop religious elements until around the 2nd century C.E. Many practitioners also meld Taoist thought with other folk practices and religions. Also, some sects of Taoism are polytheistic and believe in a number of deities and ancestral spirits that have specialized powers. These deities can be worshiped in order to gain their favor, similar to a Christian saint or Hindu deity. Finally, some believe that rituals and other formal spiritual practices are important, even essential, while others do not. Despite these various differences, at its core Taoism seeks to find balance and harmony between nature, humanity, and the spiritual world. Therefore, this chapter will explore the various concepts and symbols that are generally used by the majority of Taoists in their search to find balance and harmony, which according to psychologists is something that all people seek at some level, no matter their creed or background.

An important aspect of Taoism is the concept of *Chi*, which is the universal life force (energy of life) that gives life and form to nature and the universe. The concept of *Chi* is a universal concept that is similar to *prana* or *shakti* in Hinduism, *The Great Spirit* in Native American religions, and even the *Holy Spirit* in Christianity. The various religious and spiritual traditions have their own unique ways of cultivating this energy, yet the end goal of harnessing and channeling this divine energy in a positive and constructive way is always the same. In Chinese culture acupuncture, various herbal concoctions, incense, and even *Feng Shui* (wind and water) are used to cultivate and balance *Chi*. Many westerners are familiar with *Feng Shui* through references in pop culture but are only superficially aware of it as an interior design/decorating technique. *Feng Shui* is actually a complex system of designing buildings and spaces, in order to cultivate and channel positive *Chi*. In Japan *Reiki* massage is used as a way to cultivate and balance this life force (known as *Ki* in Japanese). In other traditions various forms of prayer, rituals, penance, and self-reflection are used.

Most people have probably experienced an ecstatic blissful state, a "spiritual high", at some point in their life, which whether they were consciously aware of it or not, resulted from the proper cultivation and channeling of this divine energy. The goal of obtaining a lasting spiritual high is usually what first attracts most spiritual seekers to the spiritual path, and the glimpses obtained along their journey is what keeps most seekers motivated to continue their journey. In order to experience a lasting blissful state, it is important to cultivate positive *Chi* by undertaking actions that cultivate positive energy, such as living in harmony with all of creation and performing acts of love, kindness, and compassion, all of which have been discussed in conjunction with the religions previously discussed in this book. Taoists believe that actions which do not cultivate positive energy can actually result in negative *Chi*, which is analogous to the concept of "sin" in most western religions and negative *Karma* in Hinduism and Buddhism.

The most important concept in Taoism is the concept of the *Tao*, which is where the religion gets its name. Where *Chi* is the force that animates life and the universe, the *Tao* is the natural balance and order that is present in the universe. The *Tao* is the pure essence, the pure potential, of everything in the universe. The *Tao* is not a personal God or deity; rather it is the natural force of balance, order, and harmony that pervades all of creation. The *Tao* is often metaphorically compared to flowing water, because it is a gentle yet powerful force that flows through all of creation. Taoists believe that the goal of this life is to conform your life to the *Tao*, which means balancing your *Chi* and your actions, with the various forces and realms of existence (the *Tao*). It is important to learn to flow with the *Tao*, because, just as a gentle river will wear down even the most resilient rock that opposes its flow, those who oppose the *Tao* will be worn down by the chaos and disharmony that their actions create.

The great Tao flows everywhere.
All things are born from it, yet it doesn't create them.
It pours itself into its work, yet it makes no claim.
It nourishes infinite worlds, yet it doesn't hold on to them.
Since it is merged with all things and hidden in their hearts, it
  can be called humble.
Since all things vanish into it and it alone endures, it can be
  called great.
It isn't aware of its greatness; thus it is truly great. [1]

If you realize that all things change, there is nothing you will try
  to hold on to.
If you aren't afraid of dying there is nothing you can't achieve.

Trying to control the future is like trying to take the master car-
  penter's place.
When you handle the master carpenter's tools, chances are that
  you'll cut your hand. [2]

Taoism seeks to provide instruction on finding the path that leads the practitioner to a state of balance and harmony with the *Tao*. However, Taoism is a very fluid religious philosophy that is meant to be a guide, rather than a strict dogmatic system. While Taoism means "The Way" or "The Path", it is said that the *Tao* cannot be taught; rather, it must be experienced. In order to experience the *Tao*, Taoism, much like Zen Buddhism, teaches that you must fully experience (live) each moment of life. In order to accomplish this great emphasis is put on becoming aware of your life experiences,

---

[1] Tao Te Ching, Chapter 34 (Stephen Mitchell Translation)
[2] Tao Te Ching, Chapter 74 (Stephen Mitchell Translation)

which means becoming aware of every sensation, every thought, and even every breath. For example, when you walk outside you should be aware of the sensations on your skin, smells in the air, visual sensations, thoughts, even the sensation of your breath entering and exiting your body. Basically, you must strive to live fully in each moment of your life. Becoming more aware of your life and everything that surrounds you will allow you to tune into the natural flow of the universe (the *Tao*). By tuning into the *Tao* you can begin to live in balance and harmony with the *Tao*, which will naturally result in peace, harmony, and happiness. Metaphorically, this is similar to the way that you tune a radio into a frequency to such an extent that static and interference become eliminated, and from the resulting clarity you can truly enjoy the radio in the way that it was meant to be experienced. This technique can be used by anyone to appreciate life more fully. Instead of mentally checking out or just trying to get through the day, make an effort to tune into your life and the world around you. Appreciate the mystery of life that each of us are blessed with.

> *What does it mean that success is as dangerous as failure?*
> *Whether you go up the ladder or down it, your position is shaky.*
> *When you stand with your two feet on the ground, you will always keep your balance.* [3]
>
> *Whoever is planted in the Tao will not be rooted up.*
> *Whoever embraces the Tao will not slip away.*

---

[3] Tao Te Ching, Chapter 13 (Stephen Mitchell Translation)

Her name will be held in honor from generation to generation.

Let the Tao be present in your life and you will become genuine.
Let it be present in your family and your family will flourish.
Let it be present in your country and your country will be an
  example to all countries in the world.
Let it be present in the universe and the universe will sing.

How do I know this is True?
By looking inside myself. [4]

The fluid and harmonious philosophy of Taoism is reflected in the essential Taoist concept of *Wu Wei* (action without action). *Wu Wei* is best described as effortless action, or acting without acting. While this may seem paradoxical, it simply means acting in accordance with the natural flow of the universe. For example: a stream flows without having to consciously act to flow, heavenly bodies revolve and orbit throughout the universe without any conscious action on their part, even plants and animals grow without having to consciously undertake any actions. Therefore, the key to *Wu Wei* is to simply act in accordance with nature, to act when it is appropriate and refrain from acting when it is inappropriate. Basically, learn to go with the flow of life.

The flowing philosophy of Taoism and *Wu Wei* is evident in the flowing and seemingly effortless martial art of *Tai Chi*, which has close ties to Taoism. In *Tai Chi*, emphasis is put on flowing move-

---

[4] Tao Te Ching, Chapter 54 (Stephen Mitchell Translation)

ments, and in combat, the opponent's energy is used against them by harnessing that energy and redirecting it efficiently. Taoists believe that through the practice of *Wu Wei*, one can ultimately find balance and harmony with the *Tao* and even positively harness its power. The concept of *Wu Wei* can be used by anyone, no matter your spiritual path or preference in order to relax and find peace. Too often people feel that they "need" to do something, or "need" to act or react in a certain way. By simply acting naturally and not worrying about what you "should do", you can find balance and order in your daily life, which will reduce and even eliminate stress and anxiety.

> *The supreme good is like water,*
> *which nourishes all things without trying to.*
> *It is content with the low places that people disdain.*
> *Thus it is like the Tao.*
>
> *In dwelling, live close to the ground.*
> *In thinking, keep to the simple.*
> *In conflict, be fair and generous.*
> *In governing, don't try to control.*
> *In work, do what you enjoy.*
> *In family life, be completely present.*
> *When you are content to be simply yourself*
> *and don't compare or compete,*
> *everybody will respect you.* [5]

In addition to *Tai Chi* and *Feng Shui*, most westerners have unknowingly been exposed to Taoism through the Yin Yang Symbol

---

[5] Tao Te Ching, Chapter 8 (Stephen Mitchell Translation)

(AKA the *Tai Chi* Disk). The Yin Yang symbol is a powerful symbol that represents the Taoist goal of finding a harmonious balance between everything, including seemingly opposing forces. The Yin Yang symbol is composed of a swirling circle divided equally into black (Yin) and white (Yang) parts; however, the Yin part contains a seed of Yang, and the Yang part contains a seed of Yin. Yin represents several forces including darkness, feminine energy, passiveness, the moon, receptiveness, cold, and death. Yang represents the opposite forces of light, masculine energy, creativity, the sun, activeness, heat, and life. Interestingly, the seed of the opposite force represents that each force not only balances the opposite force, but it is dependent on the opposite force for its very existence. After all, there cannot be darkness without life, masculine energy without feminine energy, passiveness without activeness, heat without cold, and life without death.

The Yin Yang symbolically brings the seemingly opposing forces of the universe into unity, which reflects the way that nature uses these opposite forces to create the natural balance that exists in all of creation. Taoists believe that unbalance and chaos results when any force becomes more prevalent than another; therefore, all forces (whether positive or negative) are necessary and should be balanced and harnessed. This concept can be used in your daily life in order to find balance between the various forces and emotions of life. If you find yourself in a negative situation, you should not become depressed; rather you should focus on the many blessings in your life, while putting into perspective whatever is causing the negativity.

Taoists believe that even death should not be a cause for concern, because death is balanced by life, and death is just another state of existence.

> *The Tao doesn't take sides;*
> *it gives birth to both good and evil.*
> *The Master doesn't take sides;*
> *she welcomes both saints and sinners.*
>
> *The Tao is like a bellows:*
> *it is empty yet infinitely capable.*
> *The more you use it, the more it produces;*
> *the more you talk of it, the less you understand.*
>
> *Hold on to the center.* [6]

The practices of Taoism vary but are primarily centered on the principle ethics known as the Three Treasures (aka the Three Jewels), which are *Qi*, *Shin*, and *Jing* (simplicity, patience, and compassion). There are various metaphysical, and esoteric interpretations and applications of the Three Jewels, which can be used as a kind of inner alchemy to transform your thoughts and behavior, in order to bring them more in line with the *Tao*. *Qi*, simplicity, can be applied through the practice of living and acting in a simpler more sustainable way. By using fewer resources, and requiring fewer needs, you can live in greater harmony with nature (the *Tao*). The practice of *Shin*, patience, can be applied on a personal level by not allowing yourself to become overly anxious, nervous, or angry. Patience allows

---

[6] Tao Te Ching, Chapter 5 (Stephen Mitchell Translation)

you to enjoy a happier and more harmonious mental state, which naturally balances with the *Tao*. On a societal level patience lessens conflict between humanity, nature, and the rest of creation, which naturally leads to more harmonious societies and happier individuals. The practice of *Jing*, compassion, can be practiced by reflecting the love and positive energy that surrounds each of us out into the world. Practicing compassion naturally increases your own happiness, as well as the happiness of those around you. These simple practices can be implemented by anyone in order to live a happier and more harmonious life. If enough people would implement these simple practices, the wars and strife in our modern world could be reduced, or even eliminated.

> *Some say that my teaching is nonsense.*
> *Others call it lofty but impractical.*
> *But to those who have looked inside themselves,*
> *this nonsense makes perfect sense.*
> *And to those who put it into practice,*
> *this loftiness has roots that go deep.*
>
> *I have just three things to teach:*
> *simplicity, patience, compassion.*
> *These three are your greatest treasures.*
> *Simple in actions and in thoughts,*
> *you return to the source of being.*
> *Patient with both friends and enemies,*
> *you accord with the way things are.*
> *Compassionate toward yourself,*
> *you reconcile all beings in the world.* [7]

---

[7] Tao Te Ching, Chapter 67 (Stephen Mitchell Translation)

The ultimate goal of Taoism is to live in balance and harmony with the *Tao* to such an extent that it becomes a natural and effortless state. This state of natural receptiveness is known as *Pu* (uncarved block), and is only reached when the *Tao* becomes integrated in your life to such an extent that all your actions, thoughts, and desires naturally conform to the *Tao*. In Taoism, once a person has reached this level of development, the person is considered to be a sage. A sage no longer has to "practice" *Wu Wei*, or try to implement the Three Jewels, because their actions naturally and effortlessly conform to *Wu Wei* and the Three Jewels. While many people may never reach the level of the sage, anyone can implement the practices of Taoism in order to live a happier and more harmonious life. The Taoist teachings of simplicity, harmony, and balance may be more relevant than ever in today's hectic and chaotic world. By implementing the teachings of Taoism much of the stress and anxiety that so many people suffer from can be reduced, and even eliminated. By actually experiencing each moment of life, tuning into the flow of the universe, and conforming your actions to the natural flow of the universe, anyone can experience a happier and more fulfilled life.

> *Fame or integrity: which is more important?*
> *Money or happiness: which is more valuable?*
> *Success or failure: which is more destructive?*
>
> *If you look to others for fulfillment,*
> *you will never truly be fulfilled.*
> *If your happiness depends on money,*
> *you will never be happy with yourself.*

Be content with what you have;
rejoice in the way things are.
When you realize there is nothing lacking,
the whole world belongs to you. [8]

---

[8] Tao Te Ching, Chapter 44 (Stephen Mitchell Translation)

CONFUCIANISM

The founder of Confucianism was K'ung Fu Tzu, who is better known in the western world as Confucius. Confucius lived and taught between the fourth and fifth century BCE, during a time known as the "Hundred Schools of Thought" period in Chinese History. This period of Chinese history was a time of great social, philosophical, economic, and political upheaval. Both Taoism and Confucianism developed during this time period, and both sought to bring order out of the chaos created by the period. In many ways Confucianism and Taoism are simply two sides of the same coin, because both have the same goal of developing refined and balanced societies and individuals, yet they go about achieving this goal by different means. Taoism places emphasis on personal development and refinement, in the hopes that refined, balanced, and happy individuals will make a balanced and just society. On the other hand, Confucianism places emphasis on developing a balanced and just society, in the hopes that it will lead to refined, balanced, and happy individuals in that society.

Unlike Lao Tzu, most scholars believe that Confucius was an actual person. It is believed that Confucius was a descendant of the royal house of Shang. His father, Shuliang, was a warrior nobleman in the Kingdom of Lu. It is believed that as a result of his first marriage, Shuliang had several daughters and one malformed son. Shuliang desired a son who would be able to carry on his noble lineage, so at an elderly age Shuliang divorced his first wife and began a relationship with a young woman named Yan Zheng-Zai, who may have been as young as fifteen years old at the time of their union. According to Chinese tradition Confucius was born of an "illicit union", between Shuliang and Yan Zhengzai, which could be due to the age discrepancy, or mean that Confucius was some sort of illegitimate child born out of wedlock.

Confucius' father died when he was approximately three years old, so Confucius was primarily raised by his mother. Since Confucius belonged to the ruling nobility class, he likely had some form of formal education, although he was likely largely self-taught due to the relatively limited resources of his mother. Upon reaching adulthood, he followed in the footsteps of many young noblemen of that time period by becoming a public official. It appears that his first government position was as the keeper of the Lu granary, but he quickly worked his way up to minister of justice. Confucius' rise to success appears to have been due to his being a voracious learner. Confucius took the pursuit of knowledge so seriously that he is said to have mastered the six Chinese arts of the period (ritual, music, archery, charioteering, calligraphy, and arithmetic) before the age of thirty. Confucius gave up his pursuit of governmental positions after his mother died when he was approximately 23 years old. After conducting a three year period of mourning for his mother, he began his teaching career.

During his teaching career, Confucius is said to have traveled widely in China in order to learn from other Chinese scholars, as well as refine and teach his system of philosophy. During the early years of his teaching career Confucius appears to have gathered a large following, and many provincial leaders requested his presence in their provinces. However, towards the end of his life, his influence and reputation began to fall out of favor, due in large part to his no-nonsense teaching style. Although somewhat dejected, Confucius returned to his home province of Lu and appears to have continued to teach until he died at the age of 72. Shortly after his death, his disciples compiled a work known as *Lún Yǔ*, better known in the west as the *Analects of Confucius*, which is said to be composed of the actual sayings and teachings of Confucius. Although he had largely fallen out of favor at the time of his death, within 200 years of his death, the teachings of Confucius began to spread widely in China. Confucianism has made a significant impact on the ethics, morals, customs, and laws of China, as well as in many other Asian countries. Confucianism has even begun making in-roads into the west.

The *Lún Yǔ* is considered to be the foundational text of Confucianism; however, the traditional cannon of Confucianism is also composed of what are known at the "Four Books": *Dà Xué* (Great Learning), *zhōng yōng Lún Yǔ* (Doctrine of the Mean), and *Mengzi* (Mencius), as well as the "Five Classics": *Shī Jīng* (Classic of Poetry), *Shūjīng* (Classic of History), *Lǐjì* (Classic of Rites),

Yì Jīng (Classic of Changes, also known as the "I Ching" in the west), and the *Chunqiu* (Spring and Autumn Annals). The Four Books and Five Classics are composed from the teachings of Confucius as well as from early scholarly and traditional works.

Because of Confucius' background in education and public service, he placed a high emphasis on both. Confucius was also very humanistic in his philosophy, because he believed that the perfection of man through education, self-discipline, and real-world experience was not only possible, but of paramount importance. Confucius believed that a thorough education in the arts, morality, and ethics coupled with real-world experience would allow for a continuous cycle of individual and (ultimately) societal perfection. In order to accomplish this, Confucius placed a high emphasis on training people to become public servants in the hope that they would transmit his teachings to successive generations, who would also become public servants and teachers, which would allow the cycle of continued societal refinement to perpetuate itself.

Given Confucius' humanistic approach to his philosophy, many argue that Confucianism is a philosophy rather than a religion. According to the French philosopher Voltaire, *"Confucius had no interest in falsehood; he did not pretend to be prophet; he claimed no inspiration; he taught no new religion; he used no delusions."* While Confucius would most likely have been an agnostic by today's standards, he did believe in a creative force (the *Tao*), and specifically taught the importance of religion, especially in the form of religious rituals. Also, many Confucianists believe that Confucianism is a religion, because it provides a system for personal, moral, and spiritual development, just like any other religious system. Therefore, in many ways Confucianism mirrors many eastern religions, in that it can be viewed solely as a philosophy, a lifestyle, a religion, or a combination thereof.

The teachings of Confucius are centered around what are known as the Five Virtues of Confucianism, collectively known as *Wuchang*, which are: *Li* (ritual & etiquette), *Ren* (humanity/kindness towards your fellow man), *Xin* (truthfulness, faithfulness, and sincerity), *Yi* (righteousness, honesty, generosity of soul), and *Zhi* (wisdom). For the purposes of this book, Confucianism will be explored using these five virtues, which can be applied by people of all religious traditions and spiritual paths, because like all true teachings, they are full of divine truth and wisdom.

The virtue of *Li* involves correct ritual (conduct) such as: good behavior, proper etiquette, good manners, and being polite. The concept of *Li* was very important to Confucius, as evidenced by his teaching that *Li* was composed of, "300 major and 3,000 minor rules of rituals". [1] *Li* is a somewhat abstract idea that goes beyond what many westerners think of as "ritual". While *Li* does include practicing correct religious rituals and societal customs, it is more generally and more practically correct conduct. The correct conduct would include all interactions with society, nature, material objects, and most especially a government's interaction with the governed. *Li* is

---

[1] Lǐjì: 10:22

basically the outward manifestation of our inner true-self; therefore, the more developed and refined our true-self is, the more refined and developed our actions will be. In the same way, if a government is refined and just, it will treat its citizens correctly and justly.

> *The faults of men are characteristic of the class to which they belong. By observing a man's faults, it may be known that he is virtuous.* [2]

> *The superior man thinks of virtue; the small man thinks of comfort. The superior man thinks of the sanctions of law; the small man thinks of favors which he may receive.* [3]

> *If a prince is able to govern his kingdom with the complaisance proper to the rules of propriety, what difficulty will he have? If he cannot govern it with that complaisance, what has he to do with the rules of propriety?* [4]

The virtue of *Li* can serve several important roles for those on The Path. First, *Li* can be used to ground you in your spiritual practices, such as religious services, or some sort of meditative/contemplative practice. This will allow you to stay connected and "plugged-in" to your practices. Second, since *Li* represents the outward expression of your internal self, the more developed and refined your inner-self is, the more refined and developed your actions will be. This allows you to analyze your development, because if your actions are not in-

---

[2] The Analects of Confucius: 4:7
[3] The Analects of Confucius: 4:11
[4] The Analects of Confucius: 4:13

line with your spiritual practices and beliefs, then you can identify the areas that still need improvement. Third, if you encounter someone who claims to be a spiritual master, teacher, preacher, etc., you can analyze them based on their outward conduct rather than solely on their teachings, which may save you from false teachers. Finally, *Li* can help you to analyze your government, workplace, and even the groups that you belong to, in order to see if they are acting in accordance with their purpose. If they are not acting in accordance with their purpose, you can identify areas that need to be changed or perhaps, even disassociate yourself from them, if possible.

The virtue of *Ren* involves kindness and the feelings that are associated with doing the right thing and treating your fellow man well. *Ren* is basically the motivation behind our actions. It is the "good nature" that each of us possess, but all too few of us use on a regular basis. Where *Li* is the outward manifestation of Confucian ideals, *Ren* is the inner manifestation of Confucian ideals. Confucius believed that every person was essentially good, and that *Ren* was a natural quality that everyone possesses. While *Ren* is an internal aspect of ourselves, it requires interaction with others in order to manifest. We cannot practice or develop *Ren* by being a recluse that is closed off to the world and those around us. Our interactions in our daily life provide the friction necessary to develop *Ren*, in the same way that friction is necessary in order to polish and reveal the true beauty of wood, metal, or stone.

Confucius specifically identified five relationships, in which *Ren* must be developed and used: 1) father to son – the father should be loving and kind towards the son, and the son should be respectful and devoted to his father; 2) older brother to younger brother – the older brother should be gentile and polite towards the younger brother, while the younger brother should be humble towards the older brother; 3) husband to wife – the husband should be kindhearted and gentle to his wife, and the wife should be attentive; 4) elder members of society to junior members of society – elder members of society should be considerate, while junior members should show respect to the elder members; 5) ruler to subject – the rulers should be benevolent to their subjects, and the subjects should be loyal to the rulers. While some of the relationships identified by Confucius may seem out dated in modern society, they do show how each member in a family or societal relationship is interdependent on the other members for support, and each must work in balance for harmony to exist.

> *When a youth is at home let him be filial, when abroad respectful to his elders; let him be circumspect and truthful and, while exhibiting a comprehensive love for all men, let him ally himself with the good. Having so acted, if he have energy to spare, let him employ it in polite studies.* [5]

The virtue of *Ren* can be used on the spiritual path to further develop and enhance your relationships with those around you. As you can see from the five relationships identified by Confucius, re-

---

[5] The Analects of Confucius: 1:6

spect and kindness must be present between all members in a relationship, or it will be unstable; and mistrust, hurt feelings, and anger will be prevalent. Also, by practicing the virtue of *Ren* in your relationships, you can benefit from the good feelings that *Ren* produces such as devotion, love, and respect, which are the exact opposite of the anger, stress, and anxiety that are so rampant in modern society.

> *As for the good man: what he wishes to obtain for himself, he helps others obtain; what he wishes to achieve for himself, he helps others to achieve.* [6]

> *When Fan Ch'ih asked about benevolence, the Master said, "it is to love all men". When he asked about knowledge, the Master said, "It is to know all men".* [7]

The virtue of *Xin* involves faithfulness, integrity, and doing what is right and expected of us. Confucius believed that *Xin* was a foundational requirement for a society and especially for a just government. Confucius believed that in order for a person or government to gain respect and admiration, they must first prove themselves to be trustworthy and honorable. *Xin* involves keeping our word and doing what is proper and expected of us. On a personal level, *Xin* naturally leads to peaceful and harmonious relationships. On a societal and governmental level, *Xin* leads to integrity amongst government officials, and trust and loyalty amongst the citizenry. *Xin*

---

[6] The Analects of Confucius: 6:30
[7] The Analects of Confucius: 12:22

is important, because if people do not trust one another or their government, fear and infighting naturally develops, which inevitably leads to inharmonious relationships, societies, and even violence and war.

> *When Chi K'ang asked how to cause the people to reverence their ruler, to be faithful to him, and to seek virtue within themselves, the Master said, "let him (the ruler) preside over them with solemnity; then they will reverence him. Let him be faithful and kind to all; then they will be faithful to him. Let him advance the good and teach the incompetent; then they will eagerly seek to be virtuous.* [8]

> *Hold faithfulness and sincerity as first principles.* [9]

The virtue of *Xin* can be used on the spiritual path in order to develop honesty within yourself, as well as those around you. If you give someone your word that you are going to do something, then, if at all possible, you should do what you have promised. If you have no intention of doing something, then simply decline the invitation. That way there is no expectation on you to do something that you have no intention of doing. This respect and honesty goes both ways, because if someone, or a government/group, gives you their word and fails to deliver, then you should hold them accountable. If necessary and possible, dissociate with them if they continue to break their word.

---

[8] The Analects of Confucius: 2:20
[9] The Analects of Confucius: 1:8

The philosopher Yu said: "When you make a promise consistent with what is right, you can keep your word. When you show respect consistent with good taste, you keep shame and disgrace at a distance. When he in whom you confide is one who does not fail his friends, you may trust him fully." [10]

The virtue of *Yi* involves correct action and righteousness. *Yi* is very much intertwined with the virtue of *Li* to such an extent that they are often the same thing; whereas, *Li* is the correct action according to society, *Yi* is the correct action irregardless of societal expectations. Therefore, *Yi* is the virtue and standard that all actions are judged by, even if the society as a whole may disagree with those actions. This can be a difficult virtue to understand and master, because it requires a firm understanding of the other virtues, especially *Zhi*, and how they interact with one another. While most of the Confucian virtues are primarily concerned with societal and governmental harmony, *Yi* provides an ethical standard that may go against laws, societal norms, or even what is expected of us. Basically, *Yi* can best be understood by doing what is right, no matter the consequences. History is full of examples of how a society or group may deem conduct or a course of action appropriate, where in fact that conduct or action is deplorable (slavery, genocide, segregation, discrimination, etc.). *Yi* gives each individual the duty to stand up and do what is ultimately correct, and hopefully other individuals, groups, societies,

---

[10] The Analects of Confucius: 1:13

and governments will correct their courses of conduct and actions.

> *The Master said: "A man without virtue cannot long abide in adversity, nor can he long abide in happiness, but the virtuous man is at rest in virtue, and the wise man covets it."* [11]

> *The mind of the superior man comprehends according to what is right, the inferior man comprehends according to profit and personal gain.* [12]

The virtue of *Yi* can be used on the spiritual path in order not only to help yourself, but those around you. The concept of *Yi* is very close to the Buddhist concept of "Right Action", in that we must act in ways that will prevent harm and suffering to others. Therefore, in your relationships, and especially in your leadership roles, you must take care to ensure that you are acting appropriately and not causing harm to others. If you see something that needs to be changed, you must take action to make sure that the necessary changes are made. This can be difficult, and even dangerous, but sometimes for the good of yourself and for the good of society as a whole, difficult changes and decisions must be made.

> *The Master said, "the superior man, in the world, does not set his mind either for anything, or either against anything, rather he simply aligns himself with what is right, and then he does what is right."* [13]

The final virtue of *Zhi* involves knowledge and true wisdom. *Zhi* is the true embodiment of all the Confucian virtues and allows

---

[11] The Analects of Confucius: 4:2
[12] The Analects of Confucius: 4:16
[13] The Analects of Confucius: 4:10

the true master (sage) to constantly live and act in accordance with the five virtues. *Zhi* requires a balanced and peaceful mind that will enable the true master to discern truth from falsehood. *Zhi* also requires correct action, as well as acting only when appropriate, which is very similar to the concept of *Wu Wei* in Taoism. While all people possess *Zhi*, it is a virtue that must be cultivated through practice. In order to cultivate and practice *Zhi*, it is important to use reason in order to evaluate decisions before action is taken. It is also important to learn as much as you can and expose yourself to as many ideas as possible, so that you can expand your conceptual understanding of your true-self, the universe as a whole, and ultimately God. On a personal and societal level, *Zhi* is important because it allows for balanced and harmonious relationships. *Zhi* is also an important virtue in leaders and government officials, because it requires them to act justly and even-handedly, which is essential for just and harmonious societies. The idea of creating a harmonious and just society governed by truly wise government is similar to the "philosopher kings" that Plato spoke about in his masterpiece *The Republic*.

> *The Master said: 'At fifteen I set my mind upon wisdom. At thirty I stood firm. At forty I was free of doubts. At fifty I understood the laws of heaven. At sixty my ear was docile. At seventy I could follow the desires of my heart without transgressing the right."* [14]

---

[14] The Analects of Confucius: 2:4

The virtue of *Zhi* is essential to those on The Path, because cultivating the virtue of *Zhi* (true knowledge and true wisdom) is what The Path is all about. *Zhi* is essential in not only developing sound relationships and societies, but it is essential in gaining an understanding of your true-self and your place in the universe. By cultivating and practicing *Zhi*, you will not only become a better and more confident person, but a more genuine person. If more people would truly cultivate *Zhi*, much of the ignorance and disharmony that is currently present in the world would cease. If more government and business leaders would cultivate *Zhi*, the exploitation and senseless violence and bloodshed would cease, because the ideals of peace, harmony, and cooperation would replace greed and struggles for power.

> *The Master said: "He who governs by his wisdom and moral excellence may be compared to the pole-star, which abides in its place, while all the stars bow towards it."* [15]

Confucianism is an important religion because it has helped to shape much of the morality, ethics, and governmental structures present in many Asian countries. Confucianism is similar to Taoism and other eastern religions in that it places a high emphasis on achieving both internal and external balance. Confucianism is useful to those on the path towards personal and spiritual development, because its five principle virtues can be incorporated by anyone into their path. The five principles can be adopted universally, because they contain the universal teachings of love, kindness,

---

[15] The Analects of Confucius: 2:1

and correct conduct that all religions teach. In fact, the so called "Golden Rule" taught by Jesus, *"Do to others as you would have them do to you"* [16], was taught by Confucius over 500 years prior to the birth of Jesus, *"Never impose on others what you would not choose for yourself"* [17]. If more people would practice the five virtues of Confucianism, especially the universal "Golden Rule", harmony could truly be brought out of the apparent chaos created by today's society, which would fulfill Confucius' goal of balanced and harmonious societies and individuals.

> *Tzu Chang asked Confucius the meaning of virtue, to which Confucius replied: 'To be able everywhere one goes to carry five things into practice constitutes Virtue.' On begging to know what they were, he was told: "They are courtesy, magnanimity, sincerity, earnestness, and kindness. With courtesy you will avoid insult, with magnanimity you will win all, with sincerity men will trust you, with earnestness you will have success, and with kindness you will be well fitted to command others."* [18]

---

[16] Luke 6:31
[17] The Analects of Confucius: 15:24
[18] The Analects of Confucius: 17:6

THE END

CONCLUSION

Hopefully, by reading this book you have begun to see that all religions are interconnected, in that they each share the ultimate goal of answering the fundamental questions of life that have preoccupied the human mind since the beginning of our existence: "Who am I?", "What is my purpose?", "How can I find true peace and happiness?", "Is there a God, or a higher power?", and "If there is a God or higher power, how can I connect with God?". The religions of the world are systems of beliefs that attempt to answer these questions by interpreting Divine Truth in ways that are acceptable and understandable to the various cultures and societies. The religions of the world also provide teachings to aid their practitioners in inculcating the answers to these fundamental questions into their lives in positive and constructive ways. As we move into a more global society, the religions of the world are no longer bound to a specific culture, society, or region, because they are becoming more global and accessible. Therefore, the Divine Truth contained in the world religions are more accessible than ever, and they can be used by anyone on their unique path.

Spiritual development involves discovering the answers to the fundamental questions of life, while personal development involves actually inculcating the answers into your life. For example, when you discover that a portion of the answer to the question, "Who am I?", involves an understanding that you are a creation of God, just like everything else, spiritual development occurs because that understanding leads to a greater sense and understanding of your true-self, and your connection with God and the entirety of his creation. Actually acting like you are a creation of God that is interconnected with the entirety of creation by performing acts of love, kindness, and compassion, would be personal development. Really, personal development and spiritual development go hand-in-hand, because spiritual development is a reflection of personal development and visa-versa. One naturally enhances the other.

Although the world we live in now is far from perfect, we are living in a time of unprecedented freedom and access to knowledge. Therefore, it is easier than ever to undertake a journey towards personal and spiritual development by exploring and examining the religions of the world for insight and knowledge. Educational experts have long recognized the fact that there are different styles of learners in each classroom; therefore, a successful instructor must be able to teach and provide lessons that will "speak to" the various styles of learning. In the same way, the various religions offer different lessons and styles of instruction that can be used in various ways in order to gain greater insights and knowledge. By examining the various religions you can gain insights, often unexpected, into the fundamental questions of life that you may not have identified or grasped from your parent religion, which will aid you in your path.

It should be noted that you can still be a devout follower of your faith and study other religions, as well as undertake a path towards personal and spiritual development. The teachings of the world religions don't have to replace your religion, they can simply be a supplement to your faith. The key to The Path is to seek out the answers to the fundamental questions of life by truly examining yourself as well as your beliefs. By seeking answers and examining your faith and ideas, you will strengthen your faith, much like an athlete strengthens their muscles through vigorous training. You will also be a happier and more confident person, because you will have discovered the fundamental answers to life on your own terms, rather than simply parroting the beliefs of someone else.

The religions of the world also provide a means for uniting humanity and bringing about an age of true peace and prosperity. In order to accomplish this, we must stop looking at our differences and the things that divide us and actually embrace the many things that we share and have in common. However, this will only be possible when we realize that we are all brothers and sisters created by God, and that God loves each of us, no matter what name we call him by.

As mentioned in the beginning of this book, this has been only a brief glimpse at the magnificent tapestry of world religions. Therefore, I would encourage you to explore deeper into the religions discussed in this book, as well as explore ones not covered in this book. Also, don't be afraid to ask difficult questions in order to begin, or expand, your own path towards personal and spiritual development. By seeking out the answers to the great questions of life, and inculcating their teachings into your life, you will be following in the footsteps of the greatest philosophers, spiritual teachers, and sages who have ever lived.

Good luck on your journey.

"It is the glory of God to conceal things, but the glory of kings is to search things out." [1]

---

[1] Proverbs 25:2 121

If you enjoyed this book, please recommend it to others
and visit my website:

http://www.livinginthenow.net/

4401844R00098

Made in the USA
San Bernardino, CA
21 September 2013